TIMESAVER
EXTRACTS
2

English fiction for
upper-intermediate
and advanced students

by Nigel Newbrook

with Jacky Newbrook

For Neil and Ralph

With thanks to the students of the Bell School, Saffron Walden, for trialling the materials.

PHOTOS: Page 19: Hemara/Mary Glasgow Magazines. **Page 24:** Mary Evans Picture Library. **Page 29:** Adam Crowley/Photodisc. **Page 34:** MGM/ Ronald Grant Archive. **Page 39:** Hemara/Mary Glasgow Magazines. **Page 44:** Hemara/Mary Glasgow Magazines. **Page 45:** BBC/Peter Firth. **Page 47:** BBC/Peter Firth/Sir John Geilgud (estate). **Page 50:** Mary Evans Picture Library. **Page 52:** Photodisc/Mary Glasgow Magazines. **Page 55:** Thames TV/Freemantle. **Page 60:** BBC/Peter Cushing (estate)/ Nigel Stock (estate). **Page 62:** BBC/Peter Cushing (estate)/Gary Raymond. **Page 65:** BBC/Anna Massey. **Page 70:** BBC/Zelah Clarke. **Page 75:** British Film Institute. **Page 79 & 81:** Columbia Pictures/Ronald Grant Archive. **Page 84:** ©Gail Mooney/CORBIS.

TEXTS: The publishers are grateful to the following for permission to reproduce copyright material: **Pages 19-21:** Macmillan Publishers Ltd for the extract from *Bridget Jones's Diary* by Helen Fielding; **Pages 29-31:** Penguin Books Ltd for the extract from *About a Boy* by Nick Hornby; **Pages 39-41 and 44:** Penguin Books Ltd for the extracts from *The Beach* by Alex Garland; **Pages 50-52:** The Provost and Scholars of King's College, Cambridge and the Society of Authors as the Literary Representatives of the Estate of E.M. Forster for the extract from *A Passage to India*; **Pages 55-57:** from *The Secret Diary of Adrian Mole aged 13 3/4* by Sue Townsend. Reprinted by permission of The Random House Group Ltd.; **Page 69:** Estate of James MacGibbon for *Not Waving but Drowning* by Stevie Smith; **Pages 85-86:** Extract from *Captain Corelli's Mandolin* by Louis de Bernières published by Secker & Warburg. Used by permission of The Random House Group Limited.

AUDIO: The publishers are grateful to the following for permission to reproduce copyright material: **Pages 19-21:** Extract from *Bridget Jones's Diary* by Helen Fielding, read by Suzy Aitchison, published by BBC Audiobooks; **Pages 29-31:** Penguin Books Ltd for the extract from *About a Boy* by Nick Hornby; **Pages 39-41 and 44:** Andrew Nurnberg Associates for the extracts from *The Beach* by Alex Garland; **Pages 50-52:** The Provost and Scholars of King's College, Cambridge and the Society of Authors as the Literary Representatives of the Estate of E.M. Forster for the extract from *A Passage to India*; **Pages 55-57:** from *The Secret Diary of Adrian Mole aged 13 3/4* ©Sue Townsend, 1982; **Page 69:** Estate of James MacGibbon for *Not Waving but Drowning* by Stevie Smith; **Pages 85-86:** Extract from *Captain Corelli's Mandolin* by Louis de Bernières, read by Michael Maloney, published by BBC Audiobooks

Every effort has been made to trace owners of copyright, but if any omissions can be rectified the publishers will be pleased to make the necessary arrangements.

Material written by: Nigel Newbrook with Jacky Newbrook

Editor: Thérèse Tobin

Designer: Bondi Design/Alison Bond

Cover photos: Used with permission of Universal Studios/Hugh Grant/Nicholas Hoult/Mary Evans Picture Library.

Cover Design: Bondi Design/Alison Bond

CONTENTS

For CD track numbers, see page 5

Teacher's introduction

Aims of the book

The main purpose of the book is to introduce foreign students to some famous English novels in a clear, straightforward way, whilst providing all students with the chance to practise a range of reading skills at upper-intermediate and advanced level. Related exercises also provide comprehension and vocabulary work, and speaking and writing practice. Some exercises are in a format that is particularly useful for students aiming to take the Cambridge Advanced, Proficiency and IELTS examinations. These exercises are shown in the table on page 6.

How the book is organised

There are fourteen units, each one with an extract taken from a different novel. The units are not graded and each one is self-contained, although Units 1 and 2, and 12 and 13, are linked thematically and could be done in sequence. A recording of the extracts is available. There are teaching notes for each unit, with background information, suggestions for ways of using the photocopiable material in class, and ideas for extension activities and further work. There is an answer key for all comprehension, vocabulary and Use of English sections.

How the units are organised

Each unit is divided into sections. These include:
- discussion points as pre-reading activities to raise interest in the extract
- the extract itself
- a short glossary of difficult or unusual words
- reading comprehension exercises to help students to understand the extract and to provide practice in different exam formats
- vocabulary work
- follow-up discussion on issues raised by the extract
- a writing task.

Using the book: general approaches

The teaching notes for individual units provide clear suggestions both for exploiting the material in the unit and for extension work, including role-plays and further writing practice However, teachers may want to vary their approach from unit to unit, to focus on specific task types or to provide variety.

Using the recordings

The recordings of the extracts can be played:
- before students read the extract
- while students read the text, to make reading easier
- after students have read the text and done the comprehension exercises, to reinforce their understanding of what has occurred
- at the end of the unit, for pleasure and to round off the lesson.

The teaching notes suggest which approach to use with each extract.

Using the glossary

The words in the glossary are words that students need to know to understand the text. The explanations given are for the words as they are used in the texts. There may also be other words in the text that are unfamiliar but it is not necessary for students to understand these words to understand the text. To help students to develop their general reading skills, teachers should encourage them to ignore words that they do not need, and to try to work out the meaning of other words through their context. (There are specific exercises on this skill in Units 2 and 11.)

Using the vocabulary sections

The vocabulary sections focus on different aspects of vocabulary development. Students should be encouraged to make a note of new words from these sections as this will help them to expand their general vocabulary for speaking or writing.

Using the discussion points

There are two discussion sections in each unit. The pre-reading sections get students to start thinking about the central theme of the unit, and so make the first reading of the text easier. The post-reading points extend the theme of the unit, and allow students to relate what they have read to other real-life situations. Teachers need not use all the discussion points suggested, and may like to add some of their own. Extra discussion points and/or related speaking activities are suggested in the teaching notes for some of the units.

The points in both sections could be discussed in different ways:

⟳ as a whole-class discussion led by the teacher

⟳ as a small-group discussion, where students work in groups of 4-5 and could then report their opinions and ideas back to the rest of the class

⟳ as a jigsaw activity. Students could be put into 3 groups, A, B and C, for the initial discussion of the points. They could then be re-grouped with students from A, B and C in the new group, to share their ideas. See diagram below.

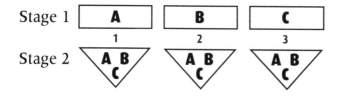

Using the writing sections

The writing tasks can be done in class or set for homework. If they are done in class, students should be encouraged to work together in pairs to produce one piece of writing as the discussion will enable them to use the ideas and vocabulary taught in the unit.

If the writing tasks are set for homework, it may be a good idea to have a short, general discussion to help students with ideas and approaches. Students should be encouraged to do a short outline plan before doing the task, and this could be discussed in class.

Follow-up work

Students may be interested in reading the book that the extract is taken from, or other books by the same author. They may also like to see the film if there is one (this information is given in the teaching notes on individual units). This related work could form the basis of a mini-project, which could be done either individually or in pairs or small groups. The aim of the project could be:

⟳ to write a review of the book

⟳ to give a presentation to the class on the whole book

⟳ to act out a scene from the book (students interested in drama might like to act out short scenes based on important moments in the novel).

CD track numbers

Track 1	Title	
Track 2	Unit 1	Bridget Jones's Diary
Track 3	Unit 2	Pride and Prejudice
Track 4	Unit 3	About a Boy
Track 5	Unit 4	The Time Machine
Track 6	Unit 5	The Beach
Track 7	Unit 5	The Beach: *Discussion and writing*
Track 8	Unit 6	The Picture of Dorian Gray
Track 9	Unit 7	A Passage to India
Track 10	Unit 8	The Secret Diary of Adrian Mole aged 13 3/4
Track 11	Unit 9	The Hound of the Baskervilles
Track 12	Unit 10	Hotel du Lac
Track 13	Unit 10	Hotel du Lac: *Not waving but drowning*
Track 14	Unit 11	Jane Eyre
Track 15	Unit 12	Dombey and Son
Track 16	Unit 13	The Millstone
Track 17	Unit 14	Captain Corelli's Mandolin

Table of exam-related exercises

UNIT	CAE (Cambridge Certificate in Advanced English)	CPE (Cambridge Certificate of Proficiency in English)	IELTS (International English Language Testing System)
1 Bridget Jones's Diary			**Reading Comprehension:** Yes/No/Not given
2 Pride and Prejudice	**Reading Comprehension:** meaning-through-context exercise provides useful practice for all three exams		
3 About a Boy			**Reading Comprehension:** Yes/No/Not given
4 The Time Machine		**Use of English:** key word transformations	**Reading Comprehension:** matching people with opinions
5 The Beach	**English in Use:** error correction		
6 The Picture of Dorian Gray	**Writing:** a review	**Writing:** a review (N.B. CPE length 300-350 words)	
7 A Passage to India	**Reading Comprehension:** multiple-choice questions	**English in Use:** word formation	**Reading Comprehension:** matching headings with paragraphs
8 The Secret Diary of Adrian Mole aged 13 3/4			
9 The Hound of the Baskervilles	**Reading Comprehension:** multiple-choice questions **Writing:** a review	**Writing:** a review (N.B. CPE length 300-350 words)	
10 Hotel du Lac	**English in Use:** error correction		**Reading Comprehension:** matching headings with paragraphs
11 Jane Eyre	**Reading Comprehension:** meaning-through-context exercise provides useful practice for all three exams		
	English in Use: word formation	**Use of English:** word formation	**Reading Comprehension:** Yes/No/Not given
12 Dombey and Son			**Writing:** presenting a balanced argument
13 The Millstone	**Writing:** an article	**Writing:** an article (N.B. CPE length 300-350 words)	
14 Captain Corelli's Mandolin	**English in Use:** register transfer		

NOTE: although students will want to concentrate on their own exam-specific exercises, they will still benefit from doing all of the exam exercise types in the units as part of their general skills training.

Teaching notes

UNIT 1
BRIDGET JONES'S DIARY
by Helen Fielding (1996)

Background information

There is a film of *Bridget Jones's Diary*.
It is usual for British people living away from home to visit their families at Christmas. The traditional meal is turkey; people usually cook a large one for Christmas Day and then eat it cold or in curries or other dishes for several days after Christmas.

Teaching notes

Write the pre-reading *Discussion* questions on the board. Ask students to discus them in small groups so that they can talk more freely.

Play the recording of the extract and ask students to listen for

⤷ **what Bridget's mother wants her to do**

⤷ **how Bridget feels about it.**

Give out the worksheet. Ask students to work in pairs. Ask them to read the extract again, check any words they need from the *Glossary* and then answer the *Reading comprehension* questions.

After completing the *Vocabulary* section, students could practise the adverbs in *Adverbs: ways of speaking* in groups. Ask them to write down three sentences each. They should then choose an adverb and read their sentences in the manner of the adverb. The others in the group have to say what they think the adverb is.

Further discussion ideas: role-play

Put students into groups of three. Tell them to imagine that one of them is a teenager and the other two are their parents. The teenager wants to buy some clothes that the parents don't like, and needs to persuade his/her parents to give him/her the money. Role-play the discussion.

UNIT 2
PRIDE AND PREJUDICE
by Jane Austen (1813)

Background information

There is a BBC video of *Pride and Prejudice*. At this time, events such as dances were important because potential husbands and wives could be met there. The word 'handsome' could be used for both men and women to mean 'good looking'.

Teaching notes

Give out the worksheet and ask students to discuss the pre-reading *Discussion* questions in groups.

Play the recording and ask students to follow the words as they listen. This will help them to understand some of the more formal vocabulary. Give them a few minutes after listening to check the meaning of words in the *Glossary*.

Ask students to do the *Reading comprehension* exercise in pairs, but check the answers with the whole class. Ask students to explain how they found the answer by referring back to the text. This will help them to develop the reading skill and make them less dependent on dictionaries. Once all the answers have been checked, the students should write the meaning of the words in the spaces in the glossary.

Vocabulary. The *Collocations* exercise (and the one in Unit 9) shows students the way some words do or do not collocate (go together) with other words, e.g. we say 'totally different' but not 'highly different' . They should be encouraged to make a note of these whole phrases, and not individual words. When students have completed the *Phrasal verbs: 'pass'* exercise, they could choose two phrasal verbs and write their own sentences using these verbs. They could read their sentences to their partner, who could tell them if the sentences are right or not.

Further discussion ideas: debate

Tell students that they are going to debate the following statement:

It was better in the old days when parents chose your husband or wife for you.

Divide the class into two groups, A and B. Tell A that they have to think of ideas to support the statement and B have to think of ideas against it. Give them a few minutes to talk and think of ideas. Then run a formal debate where they take it in turns to put a point of view. At the end they can vote for whether they agree or disagree with the statement.

UNIT 3
ABOUT A BOY
by Nick Hornby (1998)

Background information

There is a film of *About a Boy*.
It is quite common in England for people to have take-away meals – they are usually English (fish and chips) Chinese, Indian or Italian cooking.

Teaching notes

After discussing the pre-reading *Discussion* questions, play the recording of the first half of the extract up to '*sorts of life.*' in line 43. Ask students what the situation is, and how the people are feeling. Give out the worksheet and play the rest of the extract as they follow the text. Ask them how they think the boy is feeling.

Ask students to work in pairs and do the *Reading comprehension* section. Check their answers and then do some further discussion of different family situations.

Then ask students to work in pairs to do the *Vocabulary* sections.

Further discussion ideas: role-play

Put students into groups of three. Tell them to imagine that two of them have had an argument about something. The third person should try to help them to make up and resolve the argument.

UNIT 4
THE TIME MACHINE
by H G Wells (1895)

Background information

The start of the 20th century saw the beginning of a rapid growth in technological development in areas such as transport and communication. *The Time Machine* was written just before this period of innovation. People were fascinated by the thought of flying (which was still only a dream). H G Wells took this idea a step further to include the idea of travelling through time. He was very imaginative and many of his ideas in other books have become reality, such as space travel. It is interesting that Neil Armstrong landed on the moon in 1969, 68 years after H G Wells wrote *The First Men in the Moon*.

Teaching notes

The pre-reading *Discussion* points can be extended to include space travel if students are interested. Some suggestions are:
- **Do they know anything about the men who landed on the moon?**
- **Do they watch TV programmes like *Star Trek*? Why/why not? Why do they enjoy them?**

Explain that the four people in the extract are described by their jobs, not their names. Put these on the board so that students will not have any difficulty identifying who they are in the extract.
The Time Traveller
The Psychologist
The Medical Man
The Narrator

Give out the worksheet and play the recording. Ask students to follow the text as they listen. Give them a few minutes after listening to check the words in the *Glossary*, and then ask them some further questions:
- **What are the two unusual points about the model? (it was askew/ it looked unreal)**
- **Why did the Time Traveller ask his friends to look at the table? (to make sure that there were no tricks or illusions being used and that the table was real)**

‚ **Who caused the model to disappear? (the Psychologist)**

‚ **How did the group react when the model disappeared? (they were silent)**

Students may find the *Use of English* exercise difficult. If you think that they will have difficulty, then pre-teach all the missing phrases and write them on the board before you ask them to look at the exercise. Then ask them to choose the correct phrase to complete each sentence.

Further discussion ideas: role-play

Put students into groups of four. Tell them to imagine that one of them wants to volunteer to be one of the civilians on the space shuttle and go into space. The others should try to dissuade them.

Further writing ideas: story

Ask students to write a short story entitled either

My first day in space

or

The day I went back in time.

UNIT 5
THE BEACH
by Alex Garland (1996)

Background information

There is a film of *The Beach*.

It has become popular for students nowadays to travel to exotic countries, living cheaply and experiencing different cultures, either after finishing university or during the long university holidays.

Teaching notes

N.B. Make sure that when you copy the worksheet you do not give students the second reading passage (on page 44) at first.

Do the pre-reading *Discussion* task with the class.

Explain that the woman in the extract they are going to read is working class and speaks very bad English. Give out the worksheet (without the second extract) and let students follow the text as they listen to the recording. Ask students to do the *Reading comprehension, Vocabulary* and *English in use* sections in pairs.

Ask students to do the *Writing* in pairs, and then they can share their ideas with the rest of the class. Make sure that students complete the writing section *before* you give them the final part of the story. You could play them the final part of the story so that they can listen and compare their ideas before they see the text.

Further discussion ideas: role-play
Desert Island Decision

Write the following words on the board:
Torch
Penknife
Camera
Laptop computer
Radio
CD player
Compass
Shower gel and soap
Mirror

Put students into groups of five. Tell them to imagine that they are going to stay on a remote desert island for a holiday with four friends. They will be camping, and they will have to take everything they will need with them. They will stay there for a month. They have already packed the tent, cooking equipment, food and clothes. Now they have enough room in their rucksack for only three other things. Explain the meaning of any words on the board that they do not understand, then ask them to choose their three items from the list. They can add any ideas of their own if they wish. Then take feedback from the groups and find the three most popular items.

You could then discuss how easy the class would find living on a desert island, and what they would miss the most.

UNIT 6
THE PICTURE OF DORIAN GRAY
by Oscar Wilde (1891)

Background information

The 'Orleans' was either a restaurant or a gentleman's club. At that time, it was popular for men to join gentlemen-only clubs, where they would go to meet friends and socialize. It was also before the days of photography, and many people employed professional artists to paint their portraits, so this was not an unusual situation.

Teaching notes

Do the pre-reading *Discussion* with the class. Explain who the three people in the extract are, and write their names on the board. This will help students to understand what is happening in the extract.

Dorian Gray

Lord Henry Wotton

Basil Hallward

Play the recording so that students can follow the text as they listen. Then give them a few minutes to check the words in the *Glossary* before asking them to do the *Reading comprehension* in pairs.

To make the *Vocabulary* section memorable, the sentences for matching could be copied onto cards and cut out. Give a set to each pair, who can then match the cards before transferring their answers to the worksheet.

Further discussion ideas: discussion

Ask students to discuss any films that they have seen that dealt with the theme of illusion or appearance and reality. You could collect the names of films students suggest on the board and students could compare their ideas and see which films are the most popular.

UNIT 7
A PASSAGE TO INDIA
by E M Forster (1924)

Background notes

There is a film of *A Passage to India*. India used to be part of the British Empire, and a lot of British men were sent there to work. Young British women sometimes then went to India to marry them. They often lived very sheltered lives and did not join in with the local culture or traditions. Adela has gone out to India to marry, but she is interested in finding out about the 'real' India; she is clearly disappointed when she has to spend the evening in a British environment watching a rather ordinary British play.

Teaching notes

Do the pre-reading *Discussion* in small groups.

Before giving out the worksheet with the extract, you could put on the board the headings from the *Reading comprehension: matching headings* exercise. Ask students to read them and then discuss in small groups what they think the text will be about. You could then play the recording for them to listen and check their ideas.

Give out the extract and ask students to read it, and check the words from the *Glossary*. They can match the headings to the appropriate section of the text and then complete the *Reading comprehension* section.

After completing the *English in use/Use of English* section, do the *Discussion* points with the whole class and set the writing for homework.

Further discussion ideas: role-play

Put the students into groups of four. Tell them to imagine that two of them are young people planning a three-month trip around India. The other two are older family members who do not think this is a good idea. Discuss the ideas and each pair try to persuade the other pair that their ideas are the right ones. When they have finished, ask each group who won, those going on the trip or those trying to stop them. Then see whether the class as a whole is going on the trip or not.

UNIT 8
THE SECRET DIARY OF ADRIAN MOLE AGED 13 3/4
by Sue Townsend (1982)

Background information

The Royal Wedding took place in 1982, when Prince Charles married Lady Diana Spencer. She was also known as 'Lady Di'. There were a lot of celebrations on that day, and the wedding itself was shown on television all over the world.

The Singh family are of Indian origin but they have been living in England for a long time. *Land of Hope and Glory* is a traditional patriotic English song. It is ironic that only Mr Singh knows all the words.

- *Nancy Reagan* was married to President Ronald Reagan of the USA, and attended the wedding of Charles and Diana.

- *Spike Milligan* was a comedian who was a favourite of Prince Charles's.
- *Mark Phillips* was the husband of Princess Anne, the only daughter of Queen Elizabeth. They have since divorced and married other people.

The whole tone of this extract is amusing and 'tongue-in-cheek'.

Teaching notes

If you have any videos of the royal wedding, or photographs of any important wedding in your country, then you could show them to the students at the start of the lesson to get them thinking about the topic. Do the pre-reading *Discussion* points with the whole class, then give out the worksheet.

Then play the recording and ask students to follow the text as they listen.

Further discussion ideas: role-play

Discuss with the students what they think Madonna or David Beckham's lifestyle might be. Ask them to think about how they go shopping, what they eat, where they live and how they live. Then put the class into pairs. Tell them to imagine that one of them is a journalist and the other one is either Madonna or David Beckham. The journalist should interview the other student to find out as much as they can about their daily life.

Writing. the students can then write a page for a general interest magazine entitled: *A day in the life of…*

UNIT 9
THE HOUND OF THE BASKERVILLES
by Sir Arthur Conan Doyle (1902)

Background information

There are black-and-white films of many Sherlock Holmes stories available, and some more recent films. If you can't find a film of *The Hound of the Baskervilles*, then you may like to show students part of a different story, either to introduce Sherlock Holmes or as a follow-up to the unit.

Devon is a beautiful county in the west of England, which is popular with tourists. It has a large area of moorland called Dartmoor, which is rather isolated and, although people go camping and walking there, the weather can change quickly and the area can become quite dangerous if visitors do not take care. The character of Sherlock Holmes is one of the most popular in the genre of crime fiction. His fictional address at 221B Baker Street is well known and for a long time people used to write letters to that address as if he were a real person living there. There is now a small museum there.

Teaching notes

Take in a map of England and show students where Devon is. Tell them about the countryside and ask them about any similar areas in their country. Remind them of who Sherlock Holmes is. Do the pre-reading *Discussion* points with the class. Give out the worksheet and play the recording so that students can follow the text as they listen. Give them a few minutes to check the words in the *Glossary*.

Then ask them to do the *Reading comprehension* section in pairs.

Vocabulary: collocations. This exercise (and the one in Unit 2) shows students the way some words do or do not collocate (go together) with other words, in this case in a particular order, e.g. we say 'come and go' but not 'go and come'. They should be encouraged to make a note of these whole phrases, and not individual words.

Work through the *Vocabulary* section, making sure that students check their answers with each other before you give them the answers.

Further discussion ideas: a murder mystery

Put the students into groups of five. Ask each group to plan a murder story based around characters such as:

- **Colonel Brownsauce** – a retired unmarried army officer who runs a small company
- **Mrs Orange** – his secretary, recently divorced and in financial difficulty
- **Mr Right** – a young employee in the company who has recently argued with the Colonel about pay
- **Miss Hopeful** – the girl who lives next door to Mr Right

↻ **Mrs Parstbest – a widow who has her eye on the Colonel**

Tell them to decide:

A who is murdered

B what the motive was

C how the murder was committed.

They should write their story without giving away the murderer. Each group then reads out their story to the class, who have to say who they think committed the murder and why.

UNIT 10
HOTEL DU LAC
by Anita Brookner (1984)

Background information

The hotel is visited by people who want a quiet holiday, because they' ve been ill or need to get away for a while. It is referred to as a 'sanctuary'. Edith has gone to the hotel for a few weeks to allow the scandal of her cancelled wedding to die down.

Teaching notes

Do the pre-reading *Discussion* in small groups.

Before giving out the worksheet with the extract, you could put the headings on the board. Ask students to read them and then discuss in small groups what they think the text will be about. You could then play the recording for them to listen and check their ideas.

Give out the extract and ask students to read it, and check the words from the *Glossary*. They can then complete the *Reading comprehension* section and match the headings to the appropriate section of the text.

Then ask students to complete the *English in use* section in pairs.

The *Literary reference* section gives students the chance to read the poem mentioned in the extract and to see how it relates to the novel. *Not waving but drowning* was written in 1957 by Stevie Smith (1902-1971). She was born in Yorkshire and went to school in London. She won the Queen' s Gold Medal for Poetry in 1969.

Ask students to read the poem through (or play the recording to them as they read) and discuss what they think it means. (see *Answer key* for explanation of poem.) Ask them if they like the poem, and what they think of the metaphor of the title.

Further ideas for using the poem

1 Students often find poetry difficult. Discuss the differences between poetry and fiction with the whole class and explain how the ideas in poetry are expressed in much more concise language. Ask them to tell the class about any poems they particularly like (or hate).

2 Encourage students to bring a poem they like to class, so that they can share it with other students.

3 Remind students of the situation in the extract. Tell them that Edith has realised that she would be making a mistake in marrying Geoffrey. She has called off the wedding and is happy. Her friends think that <u>she</u> is the one making the mistake, and that she wants help. Ask students to work in pairs to write the poem using Anita Brookner' s reversed line. Ask them to keep to the original, but make it very clear that she does not need help. They should finish their poem with the line: *Not drowning but waving.*

4 Discuss the idea of contrasting good and bad with students. Ask them for suggestions –

e.g. Every cloud has a silver lining.

It' s an ill wind that blows nobody any good.

Ask them if they have any examples of this in their own language.

Discuss the way words can sometimes go together in unexpected ways. Ask them what kind of emotions they associate with tears. Then write *tears of happiness* on the board.

Ask students to write their own poem or short story called *Tears of Happiness*.

If they choose to write a poem, then the words *tears of happiness* should appear in the last line of the poem. The idea of the poem or story should be that the person appears to be crying for a sad reason, but is actually very happy.

UNIT 11
JANE EYRE
by Charlotte Brontë (1847)

Background information

There is a film of *Jane Eyre*.
At that time many upper-class girls didn' t go to school but they had a private governess who lived in the house and taught them in their own home. The governess was considered to be more important than the servants in the house but was not valued as part of the family. Such a job was often taken by a single woman who had little chance of getting married. Thornfield Hall was a big, impressive house that looked like a castle from a distance.

Teaching notes

Do the pre-reading *Discussion* points with the whole class.

Give out the worksheet and play the recording so that students can follow the text as they listen.

Give them a few minutes to check the words in the Glossary, then ask them to do the *Reading comprehension: meaning through context* exercise. Check the answers with the whole class, and encourage them to justify their answers from the text itself. Then ask them to write the missing definitions in the spaces in the glossary.

Further discussion ideas: role-play

In the extract, Jane does not realise that the man she has met is actually Mr Rochester, the owner of Thornfield Hall.

Ask students to imagine that Jane and Mr Rochester meet at the Hall later that evening. Tell students to work in pairs and write a short dialogue between Jane and Mr Rochester when they meet again. Tell them to think about how they might both feel and what they might feel embarrassed about. Then ask the students to act out their dialogues in front of the class. Then go to Chapter 13 of *Jane Eyre* and see what Charlotte Brontë actually wrote.

UNIT 12
DOMBEY AND SON
by Charles Dickens (1846-8)

Background information

In the novel, the firm of Dombey and Son was a powerful shipping company in the City of London. It was a family firm founded by Mr Dombey's grandfather with Mr Dombey's father as the 'Son'. When the grandfather died, the firm was run by Mr Dombey's father with Mr Dombey himself as 'Son', but when his father died there was no-one to inherit the title of 'Son'. Mr Dombey was desperate to have a son so that this family tradition could continue, and so he was delighted when his son was born, and naturally gave him his own name of Paul. Mr Dombey already had a daughter, but he considered her unimportant because she could not carry on the family name, and so he paid very little attention to her although she longed for his love and affection.

Teaching notes

Do the pre-reading *Discussion* in pairs.

Then play the recording and ask students to follow the text. Give them a few minutes to check the *Glossary*, and then ask them to work in pairs to do the *Reading comprehension* section. Check the answers with the whole class.

When students have completed the *Vocabulary: adjectives to describe people* exercise, you could write the adjectives in a list in the middle of the board. Ask the class to suggest adjectives with opposite meaning and write those on the board. Suggest that they write these on the worksheet next to the exercise. This will focus them on word formation, and encourage students to see words in connection with other words, not in isolation.

Further discussion ideas: debate

Write the statement below on the board:
The place of women in society has changed over the years, but the fact still remains that they are better off staying in the home.

Divide the class into two groups, A and B. Ask group A to think of ideas to support the statement, and group B to think of ideas against it. Then run a formal debate. At the end of the debate, ask students to vote on whether they agree or disagree with the statement.

UNIT 13
THE MILLSTONE
by Margaret Drabble (1965)

Background information

In the 1960s in England it was quite difficult for an unmarried girl to bring up a baby alone. It was difficult socially because having a baby outside marriage was unacceptable, and it was difficult financially. The novel explores the emotional problems Rosamund has while trying to manage alone.

Teaching notes

Do the pre-reading *Discussion* in small groups, then give out the worksheet. Play the recording and ask students to follow the text as they listen. Give them a few minutes to check the words in the *Glossary* and then ask them to work in pairs to do the *Reading comprehension* section.

At the end of the *Vocabulary* exercise *Idioms: parts of the body*, you could ask the students the following questions.

Who is...

⊃ ignored? (Andrew)

⊃ advising someone to keep out of trouble? (Peter)

⊃ being accused of something? (John)

⊃ involved in something? (Susan)

⊃ being encouraged? (Diane)

⊃ trying to persuade someone to do something (Adrian)

⊃ always making social mistakes? (James)

⊃ likely to irritate someone important? (Neil)

When they have done the *Vocabulary* section, focus on *Proverbs*. Ask them to work in pairs or small groups and discuss any similar proverbs they have in their own language. Are they the same or different from the ones in English? How true or useful do they think such proverbs actually are nowadays? Do they know any proverbs that are in fact opposites (e.g. nos ii and vi)?

Further discussion ideas: fluency activity – 'important moments'

Remind students that *The Millstone* is about a milestone in a young woman' s life.

Tell them that they are going to talk about their own important moments, e.g. graduating from High School, winning a prize, and so on. Put students into groups of five. Tell them they have about 7-8 minutes to find out as much as they can about each other' s important dates.

UNIT 14
CAPTAIN CORELLI' S MANDOLIN
by Louis de Bernières (1994)

Background information

There is a film of *Captain Corelli' s Mandolin*. The old couple who live in a small Greek village are likely to treat the doctor with respect, but the doctor feels that it is necessary to emphasise his social superiority by using long complicated words that they will not understand.

Teaching notes

Give out the worksheet. Do the pre-reading *Discussion* in pairs.

Then ask students to read through the list of events in the *Reading comprehension* exercise. Ask them to discuss in pairs what the text might be about, and what the possible order might be. Then play the recording and ask them to follow the text as they listen. Give them a few moments to check the words in the *Glossary*, and ask them to work in pairs to do the *Reading comprehension* exercise and put the events into the correct order. Check the answer with the whole class, and ask them to explain how they found the answer from the evidence in the text.

Ask students to do the *Vocabulary* exercises in pairs.

After doing the *English in use: register transfer* section, for further practice students could write a similar letter to the one on the worksheet. Student A should try to make their letter very formal and student B should write a very informal letter to a friend. Ask the students to exchange their letters and compare them, saying if they think the register is correct or not.

Further discussion ideas: role-play

Tell students to work in pairs. They should choose one of the follow-up *Discussion* problems and either write a short dialogue and read it to the class or act it out without a script in front of the class.

Answer key

UNIT 1
BRIDGET JONES'S DIARY

Reading comprehension
1 No
2 No
3 Yes
4 Not given
5 Yes
6 No
7 Not given
8 Yes
9 Yes
10 No

Vocabulary
Compound adjectives
i   f
ii   c
iii e
iv   b
v   a
vi   d

1 well-dressed
2 absent-minded
3 mouth-watering
4 second-class
5 far-fetched

Vocabulary
Verbs: ways of speaking
1 roared
2 shrieked
3 moaned
4 mumble

Vocabulary
Adverbs: ways of speaking
1 persuasively
2 arrogantly
3 aggressively
4 desperately

UNIT 2
PRIDE AND PREJUDICE

Reading comprehension
Meaning through context
1 a
2 b
3 b
4 b
5 a

Vocabulary
Collocations
i   d
ii   b
iii a
iv   e
v   c

1 thoroughly deserved
2 literally speechless
3 highly unlikely
4 totally different

Vocabulary
Phrasal verbs: 'pass'
1 away
2 out
3 down
4 over
5 by
6 up
7 on

UNIT 3
ABOUT A BOY

Reading comprehension
1 No
2 Yes
3 Yes
4 Not given
5 No
6 Yes
7 Not given
8 Yes

Vocabulary
Inference
i   f
ii   e
iii g
iv   a
v   d
vi   b

Vocabulary
Phrasal verbs: 'up'
i   c
ii   f
iii a
iv   e
v   b
vi   d

1 pick him up
2 doing it up
3 put up with it
4 put you up
5 held me up

UNIT 4
THE TIME MACHINE

Reading comprehension
Matching
a P
b P
c N
d MM
e TT

Vocabulary
Phrases with 'account'
1 on any account
2 accounts for
3 on my own account
4 on account of
5 gave a good account of himself

Use of English
Key word transformations
2 The time traveller was glad of the chance...*to put his theory to*...practical use.
3 The time traveller...*enjoyed nothing more than surprising*...his friends with his experiments.
4 The Time traveller's friends...*had no option but to* ...watch the conclusion of the experiment.
5 It...*was common knowledge that some of the Time Traveller's theories*...were unlikely.

6 The Time Traveller's friends found it difficult to understand his theory...*in spite of his careful ...explanation.*

UNIT 5
THE BEACH

Reading comprehension

1 Yes
2 No
3 Not given
4 Yes
5 Not given
6 No
7 Yes
8 Yes

Vocabulary
Strong adjectives

ii a
iii h
iv j
v f
vi b
vii i
vii c
ix g
x e

1 exhausted
2 furious
3 filthy
4 astounded
5 freezing

English in use
Error correction

1 was
2 which
3 ✓
4 it
5 a
6 the
7 ✓
8 it

UNIT 6
THE PICTURE OF DORIAN GRAY

Reading comprehension

1 He didn't know there was a visitor (Lord Henry) in the studio.
2 Lord Henry's aunt had told him about Dorian.
3 He forgot to take her to a club in Whitechapel.
4 That she makes enough noise for two people when she plays the piano.
5 He doesn't want to be disturbed or delayed while painting the portrait.
6 He claims to have a pre-arranged meeting with someone at 'the Orleans'.
7 Because Basil never speaks while he is painting.
8 Because he has a bad influence over all his friends.

Vocabulary
Idioms with colours

i d
ii c
iii e
iv a
v b

1 gave the green light
2 told (her) a white lie

3 the black sheep of the family
4 blue-eyed boy

Vocabulary
Idioms with 'make'

i d
ii e
iii b
iv a
v c

1 making a mountain out of a molehill
2 make yourself at home
3 make do with
4 made a name for himself

UNIT 7
A PASSAGE TO INDIA

Reading comprehension
Matching headings

1 e
2 a
3 f
4 d
5 b

Reading comprehension
Multiple choice

1 c
2 a
3 b
4 b

English in use/ Use of English
Word formation

a caution
b decisions
c distance
d pleasure
e romance
f agreement
g alterations
h considerable
i hopefully
j unsuccessful

UNIT 8
THE SECRET DIARY OF ADRIAN MOLE AGED 13 3/4

Reading comprehension

1 Because the English are described as leading the world in pageantry.
2 Because he is supposed to be a communist who wouldn't believe in having a king or a queen.
3 Because he had to go upstairs to get the spare toilet roll as his grandma was crying and had no handkerchief.
4 Because their TV wasn't working.
5 They are dirty.
6 They are going to have a street party.
7 They became drunk.

Vocabulary
Idioms with 'dead'

i c
ii d
iii a
iv e
v b

1 dead cert
2 deadline
3 dead-end job
4 dead on time

Vocabulary
Idioms with 'hand'
i   d
ii   c
iii a
iv   b
v   h
vi   e
vii f
viii g

UNIT 9
THE HOUND OF THE BASKERVILLES

Reading comprehension
1   a
2   c
3   c
4   b

Vocabulary
Ways of looking
 i   c
 ii e
 iii d
 iv a
 v   f
 vi b

Vocabulary
Idioms with 'spring'
1   sprang to attention
2   springs to mind
3   sprang into action
4   springs to her defence

Vocabulary
Collocations
ii   give and take
iii come and go
1   come and go
2   moaned and groaned
3   puff and pant
4   hide and seek

UNIT 10
HOTEL DU LAC

Reading comprehension
1   f
2   g
3   b
4   e
5   a
6   c

English in use
Error correction
 1   it
 2   of
 3   ✓
 4   what
 5   quite
 6   ✓
 7   the
 8   ✓
 9   me
10   so
11   myself
12   ✓
13   ✓
14   something
15   on
16   ✓

Literary reference
The poem describes someone who is not in control of his life, although it seems to his friends that he is. Anita Brookner has reversed the words because it is the opposite situation; Edith is in control of things but her friends think that she is overcome by difficulties.

UNIT 11
JANE EYRE

Reading comprehension
Meaning through context
1   a
2   b
3   b
4   a
5   a
6   b
7   a

Reading comprehension
Comprehension
1   No
2   Yes
3   No
4   No
5   Not given
6   Yes
7   Not given
8   No

Vocabulary
Words for 'alone'
1   alone ... lonely
2   apart
3   only
4   unique
5   solitary

English in use/ Use of English
Word formation
2   decision
3   expression
4   unfortunately
5   pleased
6   Silent
7   useless

Vocabulary
Phrasal verbs with 'put'
1   up
2   off
3   off
4   up with

UNIT 12
DOMBEY AND SON

Reading comprehension
1   He is by the fireside.
2   He is forty-eight minutes old.
3   Strict and feeling rather self-important.
4   His forehead has been marked by 'Time and Care'.
5   Hung.
6   He doesn't usually show affection.
7   Because it is assumed that he will take over the firm and will take Mr Dombey's place. It was his grandfather's name as well as Mr Dombey's name, so it is a family tradition.
8   It means the main purpose of his life, which revolves around the success of his family firm.
9   He implies that Mr Dombey places no value on daughters as his firm is 'Dombey and <u>Son</u>'.
10 She is afraid because she is 'crouching timidly'.

Vocabulary
Adjectives to describe people
1 strict
2 determined
3 thrifty
4 inquisitive
5 popular
6 sympathetic
7 eccentric
8 extravagant

Vocabulary
Verbs for different noises
1 clattered
2 struck
3 chimed
4 rattle

Vocabulary
Abbreviations
1 a This refers to a page of e.g. a letter.
2 b This could be used in a memo.
3 b This could be used in a memo or notes.
4 a This could be used in a letter or essay.
5 a This is used at the end of a letter, after the signature, to add something that has been forgotten.
6 b This is used in sections of a form which are not relevant to the person filling in the form.

UNIT 13
THE MILLSTONE

Reading comprehension
1 In hospital because she's just had a baby.
2 She wanted to wait until everything was all right, she was afraid of 'anticipating'.
3 They roared with laughter when the name was suggested.
4 The summer was quite hot so they got sun-tanned because they often walked in the park.
5 The fact that her baby loves her the most.
6 Babies don't have any choice in who looks after them.
7 They were afraid of getting the wrong answer because she's unmarried.
8 She had frenzies of weeping.

Vocabulary
Idioms: parts of the body
1 point
2 have
3 given
4 keep
5 putting
6 twist
7 Take
8 tread

Vocabulary
Phrasal verbs: intransitive
1 look up
2 get up
3 come round
4 get on
5 come off

Proverbs
i a
ii X (This means that you miss someone when they are away and your love grows stronger)
iii d
iv b
v c

UNIT 14
CAPTAIN CORELLI'S MANDOLIN

Reading comprehension
1 d
2 f
3 e
4 a
5 c
6 g
7 b

Vocabulary
Idioms with 'word'
i e
ii d
iii b
iv a
v c

Vocabulary
Idioms with 'single'
i b
ii c
iii e
iv a
v d

English in use
Register transfer
(A suggested answer)
Dear John
I'm sorry to tell you that I can't come / won't be able to come to the party at your house on Saturday. I'm afraid I have / I'll have to start work on the same day. Thanks for your invitation, and I hope that you have a good time.
Best wishes
Peter

Unit 1
Socialising

Bridget Jones's Diary
by Helen Fielding (1996)

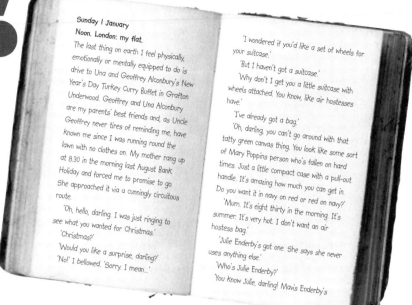

The author and the novel

Helen Fielding lives in London, and has worked for the BBC and various national newspapers.

Bridget Jones's Diary became an instant success when it was published in 1996 and was subsequently made into a highly-successful film in 2001. Helen Fielding based her hero, Mark Darcy, and some of the plot, on **Pride and Prejudice** by Jane Austen. Colin Firth, who played Mr Darcy in the BBC version of **Pride and Prejudice,** played Mark Darcy in this film.

About the extract

Bridget Jones is an unmarried woman in her thirties living in a flat in London. Her mother is trying to persuade her to go to a party that is being organised by some of her mother's old friends.

Discussion

⤳ **Have you ever had to go to a social occasion to please your parents?**

⤳ **How did you feel?**

⤳ **What was the worst thing about it?**

⤳ **Were there any good points?**

Sunday 1 January

Noon. London: my flat. The last thing on earth I feel physically, emotionally or mentally equipped to do is drive to Una and Geoffrey Alconbury's New Year's Day Turkey Curry Buffet in Grafton Underwood.

5   Geoffrey and Una Alconbury are my parents' best friends and, as Uncle Geoffrey never tires of reminding me, have known me since I was running round the lawn with no clothes on. My mother rang up at 8.30 in the morning last August Bank Holiday and forced me to promise to go. She approached it via a cunningly circuitous route.

10   'Oh, hello, darling. I was just ringing to see what you wanted for Christmas.'

'Christmas?'

'Would you like a surprise, darling?'

'No!' I bellowed. 'Sorry. I mean…'

15 'I wondered if you'd like a set of wheels for your suitcase.'

'But I haven't got a suitcase.'

'Why don't I get you a little suitcase *with wheels attached.* You know, like air hostesses have.'

'I've already got a bag.'

20 'Oh, darling, you can't go around with that tatty green canvas thing. You look like some sort of Mary Poppins person who's fallen on hard times. Just a little compact case with a pull-out handle. It's amazing how much you can get in. Do you want it in navy on red or red on navy?'

'Mum. It's eight thirty in the morning. It's summer. It's very hot. I don't 25 want an air hostess bag.'

'Julie Enderby's got one. She says she never uses anything else.'

'Who's Julie Enderby?'

'You know *Julie,* darling! Mavis Enderby's daughter, Julie! The one that's got that super-dooper job at Arthur Andersen…'

30 'Mum…'

'Always takes it on her trips…'

'I don't want a little bag with wheels on.'

'I'll tell you what. Why don't Jamie, Daddy and I all club together and get you a proper new big suitcase *and* a set of wheels?'

35 Exhausted, I held the phone away from my ear, puzzling about where the missionary luggage-Christmas-gift zeal had stemmed from. When I put the phone back she was saying: '…in actual fact, you can get them with a compartment with bottles for your bubble bath and things. The other thing I thought of was a shopping trolley.'

40 'Is there anything *you'd* like for Christmas?' I said desperately, blinking in the dazzling Bank Holiday sunlight.

'No, no,' she said airily. 'I've got everything I need. Now, darling,' she suddenly hissed, 'you will be coming to Geoffrey and Una's New Year's Day Turkey Curry Buffet this year, won't you?'

45 'Ah. Actually, I…' I panicked wildly. What could I pretend to be doing? '…think I might have to work on New Year's Day.'

'That doesn't matter. You can drive up after work. Oh, did I mention? Malcolm and Elaine Darcy are coming and bringing Mark with them. Do you remember Mark, darling? He's one of those top-notch barristers. 50 Masses of money. Divorced. It doesn't start till eight.'

Oh God. Not another strangely dressed opera freak with bushy hair burgeoning from a side-parting. 'Mum, I've told you. I don't need to be fixed up with...'

55 'Now come along, darling. Una and Geoffrey have been holding the New Year buffet since you were running round the lawn with no clothes on! Of course you're going to come. And you'll be able to use your new suitcase.'

553 words
Bridget Jones's Diary by Helen Fielding. This edition Picador 1996, pages 7-10.

Glossary

Grafton Underwood (line 4): the name of the place where Una and Geoffrey Alconbury live

Bank Holiday (line 8): a national holiday when the banks and some shops are closed

bellowed (line 14): shouted loudly

tatty (line 20): an informal word meaning in bad condition

Mary Poppins (line 21): a fictional magic character who looks after children

super-dooper (line 29): an informal word meaning extremely good (now rather out-of-date)

missionary (line 36): used here to mean persuasive

zeal (line 36): eagerness to do something

hissed (line 43): said in a loud whisper

top-notch (line 49): an informal adjective meaning the highest quality

opera freak (line 51): someone who loves opera

burgeoning (line 52): growing quickly and plentifully

Reading comprehension

1 Bridget's mother phones at Christmas to discuss the party.

2 Bridget's mother asks her immediately about the party.

3 Bridget's mother offers to buy her a suitcase suitable for air travel.

4 Bridget's mother works at Arthur Andersen.

5 Julie Enderby probably has to travel as part of her job.

6 If Bridget wants a bigger suitcase, some of her friends will pay for it between them.

7 Bridget's mother always uses a shopping trolley.

8 Bridget probably thinks that it's too soon to be discussing Christmas presents.

9 Bridget's mother is hoping that Bridget will become friendly with Mark Darcy.

10 Mark Darcy is a rich married man.

> Read the extract again and decide if the following statements are correct. Put YES, NO or NOT GIVEN (if it is impossible to say).

Vocabulary

Compound adjectives

i last

ii absent

iii far

iv mouth

v second

vi well

a -class

b -watering

c -minded

d -dressed

e -fetched

f -minute

> In line 49, Mark Darcy is described as a 'top-notch' lawyer.
> Match the following words to make compound adjectives, and then put them into the correct sentences below. There is one you will not need to use.

1 'Smart' means 'clever' in the USA and ___ - ___ in Britain.

2 Sometimes a very intelligent professor forgets ordinary details and is rather ___ - ___ .

3 The new chef at that restaurant has created some very tasty meals which look really ___ - ___ .

4 I don't believe that new employees in this company should be treated as ___ - ___ citizens.

5 The boss couldn't believe Tom's excuse about his train having an accident again; it seemed much too ___ - ___ to be true.

Vocabulary

Verbs: ways of speaking

> moan   mumble   roar
> shriek   whisper

Bridget 'bellowed' in line 14 and her mother 'hissed' in line 43.
Put the following verbs describing ways of speaking into the correct sentences. You may need to change the tense of the verb to fit the sentence. There is one verb you will not need to use.

1 'Penalty' _____ the football crowd as their star player was brought down by a defender.
2 'Help me!' _____ Mary as she fell off the cliff onto a narrow ledge.
3 'Not another grammar exercise!' _____ the students in Mr Johnson's class.
4 'I wish Professor Martin wouldn't _____ like that when he lectures; I can never make out what he's trying to say.'

Vocabulary

Adverbs: ways of speaking

> aggressively   arrogantly
> desperately   modestly
> persuasively

'No, no,' she said airily. (line 42)
The adverb 'airily' shows that Bridget's mother spoke in a way that was neither serious nor concerned. Match the adverbs in the box to the correct statements below. There is one adverb you will not need to use.

1 'Why don't you come – you'll really enjoy it, I know you will – come on, give it a try.' _____
2 'I just know that I'm better than everyone else – they don't stand a chance.' _____
3 'Do that again and I'll punch you in the face.' _____
4 'I really have to pass my driving test this time – if I don't, I just don't know what I'll do.' _____

Discussion
➲ Is it easy for teenagers to get on well with their parents, or is there a 'generation gap'?
➲ Do you feel that your parents are still trying to influence your decisions?

Writing
Imagine that you are Bridget and you are writing a letter to a friend telling him or her about the phone call with your mother and explaining the problem about going to the party. Ask for advice, and then invite your friend to visit you for a weekend next month. Give details of your plans for the weekend. Write your letter in 200-250 words.

Unit 2
...and socialising then

Pride and Prejudice
by Jane Austen (1813)

The author and the novel

Jane Austen was born in 1775. Her novels portrayed in a humorous manner the behaviour of middle-class and upper-middle-class families. The novels often revolve around the importance for young women of finding a suitable husband. The relationship between Elizabeth and Mr Darcy in **Pride and Prejudice** is particularly famous, and the BBC produced a highly-acclaimed version of the novel in 1995. There have also been recent Hollywood films of **Sense and Sensibility** with Hugh Grant and Emma Thompson, and **Emma** with Gwyneth Paltrow.

About the extract

Mrs Bennet has taken her five daughters to a dance at the assembly room in the hope of meeting Mr Bingley, a wealthy young man, newly-arrived in the neighbourhood. They also meet his friend, Mr Darcy, who is very rich but appears to be proud and unpleasant.

Discussion

➲ Have you ever been to a party or disco where you did not know many people? How did you feel?

➲ Were there any embarrassing or difficult moments?

➲ Did it take you long to decide who you liked and disliked?

And when the party entered the assembly room it consisted only of five all together – Mr Bingley, his two sisters, the husband of the eldest, and another young man.

Mr Bingley was good-looking and gentlemanlike; he had a pleasant
5   countenance, and easy, unaffected manners. His sisters were fine women, with an air of decided fashion. His brother-in-law, Mr Hurst, merely looked the gentleman; but his friend Mr Darcy, soon drew the attention of the room by his fine, tall person, handsome features, and the report which

was in general circulation within five minutes after his entrance, of his

10 having ten thousand a year. The gentlemen pronounced him to be a fine figure of a man, the ladies declared he was much handsomer than Mr Bingley, and he was looked at with great admiration for about half the evening, till his manners gave a disgust which turned the tide of his popularity; for he was discovered to be proud; to be above his company,

15 and above being pleased; and not all his large estate in Derbyshire could then save him from having a most forbidding, disagreeable countenance, and being unworthy to be compared with his friend. He was the proudest, most disagreeable man in the world, and everybody hoped that he would never come there again. Amongst the most violent against him was Mrs

20 Bennet, whose dislike of his general behaviour was sharpened into particular resentment by his having slighted one of her daughters.

Elizabeth Bennet had been obliged, by the scarcity of gentlemen, to sit down for two dances; and during part of that time, Mr Darcy had been standing near enough for her to overhear a conversation between him and

25 Mr Bingley, who came from the dance for a few minutes to press his friend to join it.

'Come, Darcy,' said he, 'I must have you dance. I hate to see you standing about by yourself in this stupid manner. You had much better dance.'

30 'I certainly shall not. You know how I detest it, unless I am particularly acquainted with my partner. At such an assembly as this it would be insupportable. Your sisters are engaged, and there is not another woman in the room whom it would not be a punishment to me to stand up with.'

'I would not be so fastidious as you are,' cried Bingley, 'for a kingdom!

35 Upon my honour, I never met with so many pleasant girls in my life as I have this evening; and there are several of them you see uncommonly pretty.'

'You are dancing with the only handsome girl in the room,' said Mr Darcy, looking at the eldest Miss Bennet.

40 'Oh! She is the most beautiful creature I ever beheld! But there is one of her sisters sitting down just behind you, who is very pretty, and I dare say very agreeable. Do let me ask my partner to introduce you.'

'Which do you mean?' and turning round he looked for a moment at Elizabeth, till catching her eye, he withdrew his own and coldly said, 'She

45 is tolerable, but not handsome enough to tempt *me*; and I am in no humour at present to give consequence to young ladies who are slighted by other men. You had better return to your partner and enjoy her smiles, for you are wasting your time with me.'

50 Mr Bingley followed his advice. Mr Darcy walked off; and Elizabeth remained with no very cordial feelings towards him. She told the story, however, with great spirit among her friends; for she had a lively, playful disposition, which delighted in anything ridiculous.

The evening altogether passed off pleasantly to the whole family. Mrs Bennet had seen her eldest daughter much admired by the Netherfield

55 party. Mr Bingley had danced with her twice, and she had been distinguished by his sisters.

640 words
Pride and Prejudice by Jane Austen. This edition Penguin Popular Classics 1994, pages 10-12.

Glossary

For words marked * see *Reading comprehension: meaning through context*

countenance (line 5): expression (on his face)

circulation (line 9): *

ten thousand a year (line 10): £10,000 earnings per year (a great deal of money at that time)

turned the tide of his popularity (line 13): *

to be above his company (line 14): to feel superior to others around him

forbidding (line 16): frightening or unfriendly

resentment (line 21): angry feeling because something is unfair

slighted (line 21): offended by treating without respect

engaged (line 32): *

fastidious (line 34): *

beheld (line 40): saw

to give consequence to (line 46): *

cordial (line 50): friendly

Netherfield (line 54): Mr Bingley has just rented a large house called Netherfield Park

distinguished (line 56): used here to mean that she was shown special attention

Reading comprehension

Meaning through context

Look again at these words or phrases in the text and choose the correct meaning, using the context to help you.

1 *in general circulation within five minutes* (line 9)

a the news passed around the room quickly
b people stood in circles for short periods

2 *turned the tide of his popularity* (line 13)

a caused him to be popular in a different way
b caused him not to be popular any longer

3 *your sisters are engaged* (line 32)

a they are going to get married
b they are already dancing with someone else

4 *I would not be so fastidious as you are* (line 34)

a I think you can't make your mind up
b I think you are very difficult to please

5 *to give consequence to* (line 46)

a it will make a young woman seem important if I dance with her
b it would cause a problem if I danced with one of these young women

Vocabulary

Collocations

i highly   **a** deserved
ii blatantly   **b** obvious
iii thoroughly   **c** speechless
iv totally   **d** unlikely
v literally   **e** different

In line 36 Mr Bingley describes some of the girls as 'uncommonly pretty'.

Match the two parts of these phrases, and then put them into the correct sentences. There is one you will not need to use.

1 Mary is such a hard worker – her promotion last month was   .

2 Mike was so shocked when he lost his job that he didn't know what to say – he was   .

3 It is   that our factory will get any more orders from that shop as it is closing down next week.

4 Although Samantha and Natalie are twins, they are   from each other in their personalities.

Vocabulary

Phrasal verbs: 'pass'

away	back	by	down
on	out	over	up

In line 53, Jane Austen says that the evening 'passed off' pleasantly.

Use the words in the box to complete the phrasal verbs in the sentences below. There is one you will not need to use. The meanings of the verbs are in brackets at the end of the sentences.

1 It was only when my elderly neighbour passed [   ] last week, that we discovered that he was actually a millionaire. (died)

2 She was so frightened by the film that she passed [   ] and had to be carried out of the cinema. (fainted)

3 Some traditions are passed [   ] from generation to generation by word of mouth. (teach someone younger about traditions)

4 He was so afraid of being passed [   ] for promotion that he worked overtime for a month. (ignored)

5 It's very easy to ignore a person in trouble and just pass [   ] without helping. (walk past)

6 Don't pass [   ] this opportunity – it's too good to miss. (miss)

7 If you see George, could you pass [   ] the information to him? (give)

Discussion

Which of these points was true in Jane Austen's day, or is true today? Are some true both then and now?

⊃ **A young woman must wait for a young man to ask her to dance.**

⊃ **A young man would be surprised if a young woman asked him out, rather than wait to be asked.**

⊃ **A young man must make sure that a young woman gets home safely after an evening social occasion.**

Writing

Write a letter to a friend, describing a social occasion you have recently attended and telling him/her about someone you have just met whom you really liked or disliked, in 200-250 words.

Unit 3
An evening in

About a Boy
by Nick Hornby
(1998)

The author and the novel

Nick Hornby was born in 1957, and lives in Highbury, London, which is the home of Arsenal Football Club, the subject of his first book **Fever Pitch**. He also wrote **High Fidelity**, which concerns the relationships of people who work in a record shop. **About a Boy** shows the development of a friendship between a thirty-six-year-old single man called Will and a twelve-year-old boy called Marcus.

About the extract

Marcus' parents separated four years previously, and now his mother has just had an argument with a male friend called Roger, who has just left. They have just ordered take-away pizzas from a local restaurant. Marcus is wondering what to do with Roger's pizza.

Discussion

➲ **What kind of food can be delivered from shops or restaurants in your area?**

➲ **In what situations might you prefer to stay at home with a 'take-away meal' rather than eat out in a restaurant?**

'What about his pizza?' They'd just ordered three pizzas when the argument started, and they hadn't arrived yet.

'We'll share it. If we're hungry.'

'They're big, though. And didn't he order one with pepperoni on it?'

5   Marcus and his mother were vegetarians. Roger wasn't.

'We'll throw it away, then,' she said.

'Or we could pick the pepperoni off. I don't think they give you much of it anyway. It's mostly cheese and tomato.'

'Marcus, I'm not really thinking about the pizzas right now.'

10   'OK. Sorry. Why did you split up?'

'Oh... this and that. I don't really know how to explain it.'

Marcus wasn't surprised that she couldn't explain what had happened. He'd heard more or less the whole argument, and he hadn't understood a word of it; there seemed to be a piece missing somewhere. When Marcus

15   and his mum argued, you could hear the important bits: too much, too expensive, too late, too young, bad for your teeth, the other channel, homework, fruit. But when his mum and her boyfriends argued, you could listen for hours and still miss the point, the thing, the fruit and homework part of it. It was like they'd been told to argue and just came out with

20   anything they could think of.

'Did he have another girlfriend?'

'I don't think so.'

'Have you got another boyfriend?'

She laughed. 'Who would that be? The guy who took the pizza orders?

25   No, Marcus, I haven't got another boyfriend. That's not how it works. Not when you're a thirty-eight-year-old working mother. There's a time problem. Ha! There's an everything problem. Why? Does it bother you?'

'I dunno.'

And he didn't know. His mum was sad, he knew that – she cried a lot

30   now, more than she did before they moved to London – but he had no idea whether that was anything to do with boyfriends. He kind of hoped it was, because then it would all get sorted out. She would meet someone, and he would make her happy. Why not? His mum was pretty, he thought, and nice, and funny sometimes, and he reckoned there must be loads of

35   blokes like Roger around. If it wasn't boyfriends, though, he didn't know what it could be, apart from something bad.

'Do you mind me having boyfriends?'

'No. Only Andrew.'

'Well, yes, I know you didn't like Andrew. But generally? You don't

40   mind the idea of it?'

'No, course not.'

'You've been really good about everything. Considering you've had two different sorts of life.'

He understood what she meant. The first sort of life had ended four

45   years ago, when he was eight and his mum and dad had split up; that was the normal, boring kind, with school and holiday and homework and weekend visits to grandparents. The second sort was messier, and there were more people and places in it: his mother's boyfriends and his dad's girlfriends; flats and houses; Cambridge and London. You wouldn't

50 believe that so much could change just because a relationship ended, but
he wasn't bothered. Sometimes he even thought he preferred the second
sort of life to the first sort. More happened, and that had to be a good
thing.

Apart from Roger, not much had happened in London yet. They'd only
55 been here for a few weeks – they'd moved on the first day of the summer
holidays – and so far it had been pretty boring. He had been to see two
films with his mum, *Home Alone 2*, which wasn't as good as *Home Alone 1*,
and *Honey, I Blew Up The Kid*, which wasn't as good as *Honey, I Shrunk the
Kids*, and his mum had said that modern films were too commercial, and
60 that when she was his age… something, he couldn't remember what. And
they'd been to have a look at his school, which was big and horrible, and
wandered around their new neighbourhood, which was called Holloway,
and had nice bits and ugly bits, and they'd had lots of talks about London,
and the changes that were happening to them, and how they were all for
65 the best, probably. But really they were sitting around waiting for their
London lives to begin.

The pizzas arrived and they ate them straight out of the boxes.

710 words
About a Boy by Nick Hornby. This edition Victor Gollancz 1998, pages 1-4.

Glossary

pepperoni (line 4): an Italian spicy dry sausage

split up (line 10): end a relationship

came out with (line 19): said

dunno (line 28): an informal word meaing don't know

blokes (line 35): an informal word meaning men

messier (line 47): here it means more complicated

Reading comprehension

Read the extract again and decide if the following statements are correct. Put YES, NO or NOT GIVEN (if it is impossible to say).

1 Marcus and his mother have ordered meat-based pizzas.

2 Marcus didn't really understand the argument between his mother and Roger.

3 Marcus' mother often seemed upset since living in London.

4 Marcus often thinks about his father.

5 Marcus had been quite keen on Andrew.

6 In some ways, life has been more lively since his parents split up.

7 Marcus had been excited about moving to London.

8 Marcus and his mother had discussed the way their life was different now.

Vocabulary

Inference

In lines 14-17 the author refers to Marcus' arguments with his mother, but doesn't give any details.

Match the words from the text on the left with the most likely subject on the right. There is one you will not need to use.

i too expensive

ii too late

iii too young

iv bad for your teeth

v the other channel

vi fruit

a a bag of sweets

b healthy eating

c making the bed

d programme selection

e coming home from a party at midnight

f a new mini-disc player

g going to an adult film

Vocabulary

Phrasal verbs: 'up'

i put someone up

ii put up with something

iii pick someone up

iv pick something up

v hold someone up

vi do something up

a collect

b delay

c accommodate

d decorate

e lift

f tolerate

g deliver

In line 10 the phrasal verb 'split up' is used, meaning 'separate'. Match the phrasal verbs on the left, which all use 'up', with the verbs with similar meanings on the right. There is one you will not need to use.

Now use five of these phrasal verbs in the sentences below. You may need to change the form of the verb.

1 When Peter arrived at the airport, Susan went in her car to   .

2 'The living-room really needs to be re-painted. Why don't we spend the weekend   ?'

3 'That new neighbour is really rude. I won't let him talk to me like that again – I really won't   .'

4 'If ever you come to London, I've got a big flat and you can stay with me – I can easily   .'

5 'I'm terribly sorry I'm late; the rush hour traffic   for over an hour.'

Discussion

➲ What ways do you know of trying to become friendly again after an argument?

➲ Would you make the first move to end the quarrel, even if it had not been your fault? Why/why not?

Writing

You have seen a magazine competition for the best story ending with the words:

Although the quarrel had been the worst they had ever had, the two friends realised that nothing would ever come between them again.

Write the story in 200-250 words.

Unit 4
The final frontier

The Time Machine
by H G Wells (1895)

The author and the novel

HG Wells (1866-1946) is famous for science fiction stories concerning future scientific inventions. He was a shopkeeper's son who eventually won a scholarship to study at the Imperial College of Science in London. He was worried that the advances in technology might eventually get out of control, and the outbreak of the Second World War convinced him that this had happened. His other famous novels are **The First Men in the Moon**, **The Invisible Man** (often filmed and recently filmed by Hollywood as **The Hollow Man**) and the **War of the Worlds**.In **The Time Machine** a man has constructed a machine capable of travelling through time.

About the extract

The Time Traveller has just explained his theory about the possibility of time travel. He is now showing his friends a small model which would be used for an experiment.

Discussion

➲ **Do you enjoy science fiction films such as *Star Wars* or *Star Trek*?**

➲ **Which aspects of science fiction films are most interesting:**

- **visiting new worlds and meeting strange creatures?**
- **the advances in technology, e.g. travelling through space in a 'transporter beam', and the possibility of these advances becoming reality?**
- **the different kinds of spacecraft and what they contain?**

'This little affair,' said the Time Traveller, resting his elbows upon the table and pressing his hands together above the apparatus, 'is only a model. It is my plan for a machine to travel through time. You will notice that it looks singularly askew, and that there is an odd twinkling

5 appearance about this bar, as though it was in some way unreal.' He pointed to the part with his finger. 'Also, here is one little white lever, and here is another.'

The Medical Man got up out of his chair and peered into the thing. 'It's beautifully made,' he said.

10 'It took two years to make,' retorted the Time Traveller. Then, when we had all imitated the action of the Medical Man, he said: 'Now I want you clearly to understand that this lever, being pressed over, sends the machine gliding into the future, and this other reverses the motion. Presently I am going to press the lever, and off the machine will go. It will vanish, pass

15 into future Time, and disappear. Have a good look at the thing. Look at the table too, and satisfy yourselves there is no trickery. I don't want to waste this model, and then be told I'm a quack.'

There was a minute's pause perhaps. The Psychologist seemed about to speak to me, but changed his mind. Then the Time Traveller put forth his

20 finger towards the lever. 'No,' he said suddenly. 'Lend me your hand.' So that it was the Psychologist himself who sent the model Time Machine on its interminable voyage. We all saw the lever turn. I am absolutely certain there was no trickery. There was a breath of wind, and the lamp flame jumped. One of the candles on the mantel was blown out, and the little

25 machine suddenly swung round, became indistinct, was seen as a ghost for a second perhaps, as an eddy of faintly glittering brass and ivory; and it was gone – vanished! Save for the lamp the table was bare.

Everyone was silent for a minute.

The Psychologist recovered from his stupor, and suddenly looked under

30 the table. At that the Time Traveller laughed cheerfully. 'Well?' he said, with a reminiscence of the Psychologist. Then, getting up, he went to the tobacco jar on the mantel, and with his back to us began to fill his pipe.

We stared at each other, 'Look here,' said the Medical Man, 'are you in earnest about this? Do you seriously believe that that machine has

35 travelled into time?'

'Certainly,' said the Time Traveller. Then he turned, lighting his pipe, to look at the Psychologist's face. (The Psychologist, to show that he was not unhinged, helped himself to a cigar and tried to light it uncut.) 'What is more, I have a big machine nearly finished in there' – he indicated the

40 laboratory – 'and when that is put together I mean to have a journey on my own account.'

After an interval the Psychologist had an inspiration. 'It must have gone into the past if it has gone anywhere,' he said.

'Why?' said the Time Traveller.

45 'Because I presume that it has not moved in space, and if it travelled into the future it would still be here all this time, since it must have travelled through this time.'

'But', said I, 'if it travelled into the past it would have been visible when we came first into this room; and last Thursday when we were here; and the Thursday before that; and so forth!'

50

'Serious objections,' remarked the Provincial Mayor, with an air of impartiality, turning towards the Time Traveller.

'Not a bit,' said the Time Traveller, and, to the Psychologist: 'You think. *You* can explain that.'

55

'Of course,' said the Psychologist, and reassured us. 'That's a simple point of psychology. I should have thought of it. We cannot see it, nor can we appreciate this machine, any more than we can the spoke of a wheel spinning, or a bullet flying through the air. If it is travelling through time fifty times or a hundred times faster than we are, if it gets through a

60

minute while we get through a second, the impression it creates will of course be only one-fiftieth or one-hundredth of what it would make if it were not travelling in time. That's plain enough.' He passed his hand through the space in which the machine had been. 'You see?' he said, laughing.

742 words
The Time Machine by H G Wells. This edition Everyman 1993, pages 8-10.

Glossary

singularly askew (line 4): noticeably not quite straight

a quack (line 17): a person who pretends to have medical knowledge or skills but has none

mantel (line 24): mantelpiece – a frame surrounding a fireplace that can be used as a shelf

eddy (line 26): a circular movement of water, wind or dust

save (line 27): except

stupor (line 29): a state in which you cannot think, speak, see or hear clearly

unhinged (line 38): mad

spoke (line 57): one of the thin metal bars which connect the outer rim of a wheel to the centre

Reading comprehension

Matching

The Time Traveller TT

The Psychologist P

The Medical Man MM

The Narrator (I) N

> Use the information in the text to match the people with the opinions (listed a-e) below. Put the person's initials to the right of the opinion.

a Time travel can be explained by relative speed.

b The model has definitely travelled in the past.

c The model can't have travelled into the past.

d The model has been well-constructed.

e It's important everyone takes the experiment seriously and doesn't think it's a trick.

Vocabulary

Phrases with 'account'

> account for
> give a good account of yourself
> on account of
> hold someone to account for
> (not) on any account
> on my own account

> In line 40 the Time Traveller says 'I mean to have a journey on my own account'. This means he wants to experience time travel personally.
>
> Put the following expressions using the word 'account' into the sentences in the correct form. The meanings are given at the end of each sentence. There is one expression you will not need to use.

1 Our teacher will not accept rude behaviour _____ . (at all)

2 The terrible weather _____ the drop in sales of sun cream. (explain)

3 When I started my own company, I was looking forward to running things _____ . (personally)

4 John said that he wouldn't be able to attend the meeting _____ his poor health. (because of)

5 Although David was by far the smallest player in the team, he _____ in the match against the champions. (played well)

Use of English

Key word transformations

> Finish the second sentence so that it has a similar meaning to the original sentence, using the word given. Don't change the word in any way, and don't use more than eight words in your answer. The first one has been done as an example.

1 The disappearance of the model was impossible for the Time Traveller's friends to explain.
loss
The Time Traveller's friends *were at a loss to explain how* the model had disappeared.

2 The Time Traveller was glad of the chance to make practical use of his theory.
put
The Time Traveller was glad of the chance _____ _____ practical use.

3 What the Time Traveller enjoyed most was surprising his friends with his experiment.
nothing
The Time Traveller _____ his friends with his experiments.

4 The Time Traveller's friends were forced into watching the conclusion of the experiment.
option
The Time Traveller's friends _____ watch the conclusion of the experiment.

5 They all knew that the Time Traveller had some unlikely theories.
common
It _____ were unlikely.

6 The Time Traveller's friends found it difficult to understand his theory although he explained it very carefully.
spite
The Time Traveller's friends found it difficult to understand his theory _____ _____ explanation.

Discussion

➲ Do you think it will ever be possible to travel into the future?
➲ How far into the future would you like to travel? What might life be like then?

Writing

You have seen the following announcement of a competition, and have decided to enter.

FIRST STUDENT IN SPACE!

The Space Centre in the USA has one free place available on the next 'Space Shuttle' Mission for a student who is interested in space travel. Write a letter to the Director of the Space Centre, stating what appeals to you about space travel and explaining why you would be the best student to be selected for this mission.

Write your letter in 200-250 words.

Unit 5

Exotic places

The Beach
by Alex Garland (1996)

The author and the novel

Alex Garland was born in London in 1970 and studied History of Art at Manchester University. He has frequently travelled in Southeast Asia, which is the setting for **The Beach**. The book was an instant best seller when it was published in 1996, and was subsequently made into a successful film with Leonardo di Caprio in the main role. **The Beach** revolves around a small group of Western travellers in Thailand and their attempt to find a kind of paradise on a remote island.

About the extract

A young Englishman, Richard, has just arrived in Thailand, and is staying at a guest house in Khao San Road.

Discussion

꩜ **Do you prefer to go on holiday with your family, a group of friends, one friend or alone? Why?**

꩜ **Which country would you like to visit for your next foreign holiday? Why?**

꩜ **What do you do on the first day in a new place?**

After breakfast I decided to have a wander around Bangkok, or at the very least, the streets around Khao San. I paid for my food and headed for my room to get some more cash, thinking I might need to get a taxi somewhere.

5   There was an old woman at the top of the stairs, cleaning the windows with a mop. Water was pouring off the glass and down to the floor. She was completely soaked, and as the mop lurched around the windows it skimmed dangerously close to a bare light-bulb hanging from the ceiling.

'Excuse me,' I said, checking I wasn't about to be included in the
10   puddle of potential death that was expanding on the floor. She turned

around. 'That light is dangerous with the water.'

'Yes,' she replied. Her teeth were either black and rotten or yellow as mustard: it looked like she had a mouth full of wasps. 'Hot-hot.' She deliberately brushed the light-bulb with the edge of her mop. Water

15 boiled angrily on the bulb, and a curl of steam rose up to the ceiling.

I shuddered. 'Careful!... The electricity could kill you.'

'Hot.'

'Yes, but...' I paused, seeing that I was on to a non-starter language-wise, then decided to soldier on.

20 I glanced around. We were the only two people on the landing.

'OK, look.'

I began a short mime of mopping down the windows before sticking my imaginary mop into the light. Then I began jerking around, electrocuted.

25 She placed a shrivelled hand on my arm to stop my convulsions.

'Hey, man,' she drawled in a voice too high-pitched to describe as mellow. 'It cool.'

I raised my eyebrows, not sure I'd heard her words correctly.

'Chill,' she added. 'No worry.'

30 'Right,' I said, trying to accept the union of Thai crone and hippy jargon with grace. She'd clearly been working on the Khao San Road a long time. Feeling chided, I started walking down the corridor to my room.

'Hey,' she called after me. 'Le'er for you, man.'

I stopped. 'A what?'

35 'Le'er.'

'...Letter?'

'*Le'er*! On you *door*!'

I nodded my thanks, wondering how she knew which was my room, and continued down the corridor. Sure enough, taped to my door was an

40 envelope. On it was written 'Here is a map' in laboured joined-up writing. I was still so surprised at the old woman's strange vocabulary that I took the letter in my stride.

The woman watched me from the other end of the corridor, leaning on her mop. I held up the envelope. 'Got it. Thanks. Do you know who it's

45 from?'

She frowned, not understanding the question.

'Did you see anybody put this here?'

I started another little mime and she shook her head.

'Well, anyway, thanks.'

50 'No worry,' she said, and returned to her windows.

A couple of minutes later I was sitting on my bed with the ceiling fan chilling the back of my neck, and the map in my hands. Beside me the empty envelope rustled under the breeze. Outside, the old woman clanked up the stairs with her mop and bucket to the next level.

55   The map was beautifully coloured in. The islands' perimeters were drawn in green biro and little blue pencil waves bobbed in the sea. A compass sat in the top-right-hand corner, carefully segmented into sixteen points, each with an arrow tip and appropriate bearing. At the top of the map it read 'Gulf of Thailand' in thick red marker. A thinner red pen had

60   been used for the islands' names.

It was so carefully drawn that I had to smile. It reminded me of geography homework and tracing paper. A brief memory surfaced of my teacher handing out exercise books and sarcastic quips.

'So who's it from?' I muttered, and checked the envelope once more for

65   an accompanying note of explanation. It was empty.

Then, on one of a small cluster of islands I noticed a black mark. An X mark. I looked closer. Written underneath in tiny letters was the word 'Beach'.

I wasn't sure exactly what I was going to say to him. I was curious, partly,

70   just wanting to know what the deal was with this beach of his. Also I was pissed off. It seemed like the guy was set on invading my holiday, freaking me out by hissing through the mosquito netting in the middle of the night and leaving strange maps for me to discover.

743 words
The Beach by Alex Garland. This edition Viking 1999, pages 13-15.

Glossary

mop (line 6): a long stick with pieces of thick material or sponge on the end, used for cleaning

lurched (line 7): moved suddenly forwards or sideways in an uncontrolled way

skimmed (line 8): moved quickly, close to the surface of something

shuddered (line 16): shook uncontrollably for a very short time out of fear or a feeling that something was unpleasant

non-starter (line 18): something that has no chance of success

soldier on (line 19): continue with something that is difficult

shrivelled (line 25): old, dry and wrinkled

drawled (line 26): spoke in a slow, unclear way with long vowel sounds

mellow (line 27): pleasant and smooth

crone (line 30): an ugly and unpleasant old woman

chided (line 32): criticised or told off for doing something wrong

took ... in my stride (line 41): was not upset

sarcastic quips (line 63): jokes that are made by saying the opposite of what you really mean

pissed off (line 71): a slang word meaning fed up

freaking me out (line 71): a slang expression meaning making me feel uncomfortable

Reading comprehension

1 The woman might be involved in a dangerous activity.

2 The woman's use of words is easy to understand.

3 The woman should probably stop work and have a rest.

4 It was surprising that the old woman knew which was the narrator's bedroom.

5 The old woman often gives messages to guests.

6 It would be difficult to find anywhere using this map.

7 This map made the narrator remember certain lessons at school.

8 The narrator had mixed feelings after receiving the map.

Vocabulary

Strong adjectives

i angry *d*
ii cold
iii dirty
iv hungry
v large
vi sad
vii small
viii surprised
ix tired
x wet

a freezing
b depressed
c amazed
d furious
e soaked
f enormous
g exhausted
h filthy
i tiny
j starving

Now put a suitable strong adjective in the following sentences.

1 After walking round London all day, I felt completely _____ and went straight to bed.

2 Although my teacher is not normally an angry man, he was absolutely _____ when I came late for the third time running.

3 Because the flat hadn't been cleaned for several months, it was really much too _____ for a young married couple with a young baby.

4 The students had expected their teacher to know all the answers, and were really _____ when she confused the second and third conditionals.

5 When the central heating stopped working in the middle of the winter, my flat was absolutely _____ .

English in use

Error correction

Read the passage below, which is based on the text. Some of the lines are correct but some have a word that should not be there.

Put a tick (✓) if the sentence is correct. If there is an extra word, write this word at the end of the line, and then check your answers with the original text.

0 A couple of minutes later I was sitting on my bed

1 with the ceiling fan was chilling the back of my neck, and the map in my hands. _____

2 Beside me the empty envelope which rustled under the breeze. _____

3 Outside, the old woman clanked up the stairs with her mop and bucket to the next level. _____

4 The map was beautifully coloured it in. The islands' perimeters were drawn _____

5 in green biro and a little blue pencil waves bobbed in the sea. A compass sat in the _____

6 top-right-hand corner, carefully segmented into the sixteen points, each with _____

7 an arrow tip and appropriate bearing. At the top of the map it read 'Gulf of Thailand' _____

8 in thick red marker. A thinner red pen it had been used for the islands' names. _____

Discussion and writing

Discuss

➲ **why you think the narrator might have been given the map.**

➲ **what you think will happen when the narrator finds the man who has sent him the map.**

Now write the next paragraph of the story. When you have finished, compare your version with a partner, and then both read the next paragraph, which you will be given. Discuss how close your ideas were to the actual text and what you think might happen next.

Discussion and writing

His door was unlocked, the padlock missing. I listened outside for a
minute before knocking, and when I did the door swung open.

In spite of the newspaper pages stuck over the windows, there was
enough light coming in for me to see. The man was lying on the bed,

5 looking up at the ceiling. I think he'd slit his wrists. Or it could have been
his neck. In the gloom, with so much blood splashed about, it was hard to
tell what he'd slit. But I knew he'd done the cutting: there was a knife in
his hand.

I stood still, gazing at the body for a couple of moments. Then I went to

10 get help.

117 words
The Beach by Alex Garland. This edition Viking 1999, page 15.

Glossary

padlock (line 1): a small lock

gloom (line 6): darkness

slit (line 5): cut

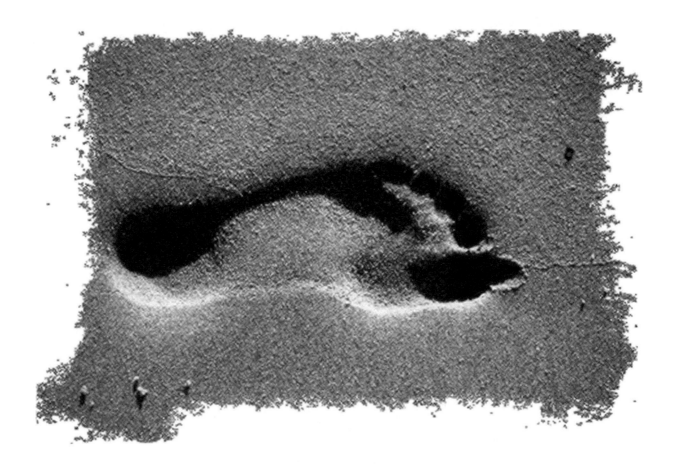

Unit 6
Appearance and reality

The Picture of Dorian Gray
by Oscar Wilde (1891)

The author and the novel

Oscar Wilde was born in Ireland in 1854 and died in France in 1900. He wrote various famous plays such as **The Importance of Being Earnest** and **An Ideal Husband**. **The Picture of Dorian Gray** is his only novel and concerns a young man who has his picture painted. He wishes that he could stay young and that his image in the painting would grow old instead. His wish comes true, but his youthful appearance is like a mask which conceals his evil deeds.

About the extract

This comes from early in the novel, when Dorian is sitting for his painting in the studio of the artist, Basil Hallward. They are talking while Basil is painting, when Lord Henry, one of Basil's friends, arrives.

Discussion

➲ **Do you like having your photograph taken? If so, do you prefer formal or informal situations? Why?**

➲ **Have you seen any paintings or old photographs of people from a hundred years ago? Did they look happy? Were they young or old?**

'Oh, I am tired of sitting, and I don't want a life-sized portrait of myself,' answered Dorian, swinging round on the music-stool, in a wilful, petulant manner. When he caught sight of Lord Henry, a faint blush coloured his cheeks for a moment, and he started up. 'I beg your pardon,
5   Basil, but I didn't know you had anyone with you.'

'This is Lord Henry Wotton, an old Oxford friend of mine. I have just been telling him what a capital sitter you were, and now you have spoiled everything.'

'You have not spoiled my pleasure in meeting you, Mr Gray,' said Lord
10   Henry, stepping forward and extending his hand. 'My aunt has often
spoken to me about you. You are one of her favourites, and, I am afraid,
one of her victims also.'

'I am in Lady Agatha's black books at present,' answered Dorian, with
a funny look of penitence. 'I promised to go to a club in Whitechapel with
15   her last Tuesday, and I really forgot all about it. We were to have played a
duet together – three duets, I believe. I don't know what she will say to
me. I am far too frightened to call.'

'Oh, I will make your peace with my aunt. She is quite devoted to you.
And I don't think it really matters about your not being there. The
20   audience probably thought it was a duet. When Aunt Agatha sits down to
the piano she makes quite enough noise for two people.'

'That is very horrid to her, and not very nice to me,' answered Dorian,
laughing.

The painter had been busy mixing his colours and getting his brushes
25   ready. He was looking worried, and when he heard Lord Henry's last
remark he glanced at him, hesitated for a moment, and then said 'Henry, I
want to finish this picture today. Would you think it awfully rude of me if
I asked you to go away?'

Lord Henry smiled, and looked at Dorian Gray. 'Am I to go, Mr Gray?'
30   he asked.

'Oh, please don't, Lord Henry. I see that Basil is in one of his sulky
moods; and I can't bear him when he sulks.'

Basil Hallward bit his lip. 'If Dorian wishes it, of course you must stay.
Dorian's whims are laws to everybody, except himself.'

35   Lord Henry took up his hat and gloves. 'You are very pressing, Basil,
but I am afraid I must go. I have promised to meet a man at the Orleans.
Goodbye, Mr Gray. Come and see me some afternoon in Curzon Street. I
am nearly always at home at five o'clock. Write to me when you are
coming. I should be sorry to miss you.'

40   'Basil,' cried Dorian Gray, 'if Lord Henry Wotton goes I shall go too.
You never open your lips while you are painting, and it is horribly dull
standing on a platform and trying to look pleasant. Ask him to stay. I insist
upon it.'

'Stay, Henry, to oblige Dorian, and to oblige me,' said Basil, gazing
45   intently at his picture. 'It is quite true, I never talk when I am working,
and never listen either, and it must be dreadfully tedious for my
unfortunate sitters, I beg you to stay.'

'But what about my man at the Orleans?'

The painter laughed. 'I don't think there will be any difficulty about
50 that. Sit down again, Henry. And now Dorian, get up on the platform and
don't move about too much, or pay any attention to what Lord Henry says.
He has a very bad influence over all his friends, with the single exception
of myself.'

605 words
The Picture of Dorian Gray by Oscar Wilde. This edition Wordsworth Classics 1992, pages 25-28.

Glossary

wilful (line 2): continuing to do what you want, although you have been told to stop

petulant (line 3): behaving in an angry way for no reason, like a child

capital (line 7): an adjective used in an old fashioned way to mean good

penitence (line 14): feeling sorry

sulky (line 31): showing that you are angry about something by looking angry and being silent

whims (line 34): sudden feelings that you would like to do something

Reading comprehension

1 Why did Dorian 'blush' in line 3?

2 How does Lord Henry know of Dorian Gray?

3 Why is Lady Agatha not pleased with Dorian?

4 What is the rather impolite comment made about Aunt Agatha?

5 Why does Basil (the painter) ask Lord Henry to leave?

6 What reason does Lord Henry give for having to leave?

7 Why is it usually boring for the person being painted by Basil?

8 Why does Basil tell Dorian not to listen to Lord Henry?

Vocabulary

Idioms with colours

In line 13 Dorian says 'I am in Lady Agatha's black books', meaning that she has some reason for being angry with him at that moment.

Match the two halves of the sentences below which use idioms based on colours.

i The black sheep of the family

ii A blue-eyed boy

iii If you give someone the green light

iv If you lay out the red carpet

v Someone who tells a white lie

a you give someone special treatment.

b is trying to avoid hurting someone by not telling the truth.

c is someone's favourite, probably because he is so successful.

d is the person who is considered to bring disgrace rather than honour.

e you give them permission to do something

Now use four of these idioms in the sentences below. You may need to change the form of the verb.

1 The boss _____ to the proposed changes in the structure of the company.

2 John didn't like to tell Mary that he really hated her new dress, so he _____ .

3 Everyone in the Jones family was successful and famous apart from Uncle Jim, who was in prison. He really was _____ .

4 Michael was top of his class, the winner of the school race, and helped old people in his spare time. In fact, he was a real _____ .

Vocabulary

Idioms with 'make'

In line 18, Lord Henry says 'Oh, I will make ... peace with my aunt'. This means trying to become friendly again after a disagreement.

Match the two halves of the sentences below, which use idioms based on 'make'.

i If you make do with something

ii If you make heavy weather of something

iii If you make a mountain out of a molehill

iv If you make a name for yourself

v If you make yourself at home

a you become famous.

b you give a lot of attention to an unimportant matter.

c you feel as comfortable as if you were in your own house.

d you accept something of inferior quality (possibly because there's no alternative).

e you find it very difficult to do something.

Now use four of these idioms in the sentences below. You may need to change the form of the verb.

1 'I've only spilt a little water on the carpet. Don't keep on about it – it's such a small thing. You're
_____ .'

2 'Help yourself to a glass of wine and something to eat. Don't wait to be asked. Just
_____ .'

3 During the electricians' strike in the winter, we couldn't use the cooker and so we had to
_____ cold food and drinks..

4 Charles Dickens had previously been unknown, but he really
_____ when **The Pickwick Papers** was published in 1836.

Discussion

At the end of the novel, Dorian is found dead, looking old and ugly, whilst the portrait shows his 'youth and beauty'. The difference between appearance and reality is also a theme in films such as **The Truman Show**, **Pleasantville**, **The Game** and **The Matrix**.

➲ **Have you seen any of these films?**

➲ **What did you like or dislike about them?**

Writing

Write a review of a novel you have read. Describe the main characters and say what happens. Say whether you would recommend it and give your reasons. Use 200-250 words.

Unit 7
Worlds apart

A Passage to India
by E M Forster
(1924)

The author and the novel

E M Forster was born in London in 1879 and studied and lectured at Cambridge University. His other well-known novels are **Howard's End** and **A Room with a View**. They all concern personal relations and the problem of communication between different classes and cultures. **A Passage to India** is about Mrs Moore's and Miss Adela Quested's visit to India over 80 years ago. At that time the Indians called the English gentlemen 'sahibs' and the English ladies 'memsahibs'.

About the extract

Mrs Moore has just arrived in India to visit her son, Ronny, who is the City Magistrate, an important legal position. Adela Quested has accompanied Mrs Moore to India and it is expected that she will marry Ronny in due course. They are attending a social evening at the club for English residents where a play called Cousin Kate is in progress. Mr Turton, an official with the title of 'the Collector', is also present. (The extract has been divided into five sections)

Discussion

⊃ **Why do people like to visit countries far away from their own?**

⊃ **What difficulties might you come across in the first few days of your visit to such a different country?**

---

1 The third act of *Cousin Kate* was well advanced by the time Mrs Moore re-entered the Club. Windows were barred, lest the servants should see their memsahibs acting, and the heat was consequently immense. One electric fan revolved like a wounded bird, another was out of order. Disinclined to return

5 to the audience, she went into the billiard-room, where she was greeted by
'I want to see the *real* India'. This was Adela Quested, the queer, cautious girl
whom Ronny had commissioned her to bring from England, and Ronny was
her son, also cautious, whom Miss Quested would probably though not
certainly marry, and she herself was an elderly lady.

10 **2** 'I want to see it too, and I only wish we could. Apparently the Turtons
will arrange something for next Tuesday.'
    'It'll end in an elephant ride, it always does. Look at this evening.
Cousin Kate! Imagine, *Cousin Kate*! But where have you been off to? Did you
succeed in catching the moon in the Ganges?'
15 The two ladies had happened, the night before, to see the moon's
reflection in a distant channel of the stream. The water had drawn it out, so
that it had seemed larger than the real moon, and brighter, which had pleased
them.
    'I went to the mosque, but I did not catch the moon.'
20 'The angle would have altered – she rises later.'
    'Later and later,' yawned Mrs Moore, who was tired after her walk. 'Let
me think – we don't see the other side of the moon out here, no.'

3 'Come, India's not as bad as all that,' said a pleasant voice. 'Other side of
the earth, if you like, but we stick to the same old moon.' Neither of them
25 knew the speaker, nor did they ever see him again. He passed with his
friendly word through red-brick pillars into the darkness.

4 'We aren't even seeing the other side of the world; that's our complaint,'
said Adela. Mrs Moore agreed; she too was disappointed at the dullness of
their new life. They had made such a romantic voyage across the
30 Mediterranean and through the sands of Egypt to the harbour of Bombay, to
find only a gridiron of bungalows at the end of it. But she did not take the
disappointment as seriously as Miss Quested; for the reason that she was
forty years older, and had learned that life never gives us what we want at the
moment that we consider appropriate. Adventures do occur, but not
35 punctually. She said again that she hoped that something interesting
would be arranged for next Tuesday.

5 'Have a drink,' said another pleasant voice. 'Mrs Moore – Miss Quested
– have a drink, have two drinks.' They knew who it was this time – the
Collector, Mr Turton, with whom they had dined. Like themselves, he had
40 found the atmosphere of *Cousin Kate* too hot. Ronny, he told them, was

stage-managing in place of Major Callendar, whom some native subordinate or other had let down, and doing it very well; then he turned to Ronny's other merits, and in quiet, decisive tones said much that was flattering. It wasn't that the young man was particularly good at the games

45 or the lingo, or that he had much notion of the Law, but – apparently a large but – Ronny was dignified.

562 words
A Passage to India by E M Forster. This edition Penguin Books 1936, pages 42-43

Glossary

lest (line 2): in case, to make sure that something will not happen

billiard room (line 5): a place to play billiards, a game like pool or snooker

commissioned (line 7): asked

gridiron of bungalows (line 31): houses with a ground floor only, arranged in organised lines

let down (line 42): not done what they had promised to do

lingo (line 45): an informal word meaning a language, usually foreign

Reading comprehension

Matching headings

a A walk in the moonlight

b Discussing someone's good points

c A problem with servants' pay

d Expectation and reality

e A mother, a son and a potential fiancée

f A passing stranger

> There are five sections to the text. Choose the most suitable heading for each section from the list of headings below. There is one you will not need to use.

Reading Comprehension

Multiple choice

> In the following four questions, choose the best answer a, b, or c.

1 Adela Quested

a wants to return to the audience.
b likes being with English people at the Club.
c would like to get a clearer idea of the country and its people.

2 The two ladies

a would like to see the reflection of the moon in the river.
b would like to go on an elephant ride.
c are impressed by *Cousin Kate*.

3 Mrs Moore

a is forty years old.
b was able to accept her disappointment about India quite easily.
c is not a punctual person.

4 Mr Turton

a was acting as stage manager.
b did not want to see the rest of *Cousin Kate*.
c was not particularly good at games.

English in use/Use of English

Word formation

> cautious   decisive   distant
> pleasant   romantic
>
> agree   alter   consider
> hope   succeed

Look again at these five adjectives and five verbs which have been taken from the text.

Each word is placed at the end of a new sentence below. Change the form of the word to fit the new sentence. You will need to make nouns, adjectives or adverbs. The first one has been done as an example.

1 The police officer told the motorist to drive with *caution* in future. (cautious)

2 Choosing the person to marry is one of the most important _____ you will ever make. (decisive)

3 In the 1500 metres final, the _____ between the first two runners was only half a metre. (distant)

4 It was really a _____ to see you again after so many years. (pleasant)

5 Novels about adventure and _____ in an exotic location are always popular. (romantic)

6 It took the committee five hours to reach _____ on the new proposal. (agree)

7 Are you going to make any _____ to that old house, now that you've bought it? (alter)

8 There is a _____ difference in price between buying a wedding dress and hiring one. (consider)

9 'The exam shouldn't be too difficult.' said the student _____ . (hope)

10 Captain Scott wanted to reach the South Pole first, but he was _____ . (succeed)

Discussion

⊃ **If you lived in a totally different foreign country for several years, what would you miss most about your own country?**

⊃ **Would you prefer to visit several countries for a short time or one country for a longer time? Why?**

Writing

An English teacher you know is planning to bring a group of English teenagers to visit your town for two weeks in the summer. Write a letter to him/her giving advice on how best to prepare for the trip, what to bring with them and how to avoid problems. Give some details of the places of interest to be visited. Write about 200-250 words.

Unit 8
A memorable day

The Secret Diary of Adrian Mole aged 13 3/4
by Sue Townsend (1982)

The author and the novel

Sue Townsend was born in 1946 in Leicester, and has written various plays and dramas for the BBC. **The Secret Diary of Adrian Mole** was an instant success when it was published in 1982. Adrian Mole is a teenage boy who keeps a diary recording daily events in his life concerning himself, his family and his friends. There have been various sequels, the most recent being **The Cappuccino Years**, all written in diary form.

About the extract

This diary entry describes the Royal Wedding of Prince Charles to Lady Diana Spencer in 1981 and what Adrian's family did on that day. There was a great deal of interest in the wedding and most people watched it on television.

Discussion

➲ Is there a royal family in your country? Did you use to have one? Do magazines have photos and articles about them, and/or about the British royal family?

➲ Has there been a wedding in your country recently of a famous person such as a film star, a well-known sports person or a pop singer? Was there a lot of coverage in the newspapers and on TV?

Wednesday July 29th
ROYAL WEDDING DAY!!!!

How proud I am to be English!

Foreigners must be as sick as pigs!

5   We truly lead the world when it comes to pageantry! I must admit to having tears in my eyes when I saw all the cockneys cheering heartily all the rich, well-dressed, famous people going by in carriages and Rolls Royces.

Grandma and Bert Baxter came to our house to watch the wedding
10 because we have got a twenty-four-inch colour. They got on all right at
first but then Bert remembered he was a communist and started saying
anti-royalist things like 'the idle rich' and 'parasites', so grandma sent him
back to the Singh's colour portable.

Prince Charles looked quite handsome in spite of his ears. His brother
15 is dead good-looking; it's a shame they couldn't have swapped heads just
for the day. Lady Diana melted my heartstrings in her dirty white dress.
She even helped an old man up the aisle. I thought it was very kind of her
considering it was her wedding day. Loads of dead famous people were
there. Nancy Reagan, Spike Milligan, Mark Phillips, etc., etc. The Queen
20 looked a bit jealous. I expect it was because people weren't looking at *her*
for a change.

The Prince had remembered to take the price ticket off his shoes. So
that was one worry off my mind.

When the Prince and Di exchanged rings my grandma started to cry.
25 She hadn't brought her handkerchief so I went upstairs to get the spare
toilet roll. When I came downstairs they were married. So I missed the
Historic moment of their marriage!

I made a cup of tea during all the boring musical interval, but I was
back in time to see that Kiwi woman singing. She has certainly got a good
30 pair of lungs on her.

Grandma and I were just settling down to watch the happy couple's
triumphant ride back to the palace when there was a loud banging on the
front door. We ignored it so my father was forced to get out of bed and
open the door. Bert and Mr and Mrs Singh and all the little Singhs came in
35 asking for sanctuary. Their telly had broken down! My grandma tightened
her lips, she is not keen on foreign people. My father let them all in, and
then took grandma home in the car. The Singhs and Bert gathered round
the television talking in Hindi.

Mrs Singh handed round some little cornish pasties. I ate one of them
40 and had to drink a gallon of water. I thought my mouth had caught fire!
They were not cornish pasties.

We watched television until the happy couple left Victoria Station on a
very strange-looking train. Bert said it was only strange-looking because it
was clean.

45 Mrs O'Leary came in and asked if she could borrow our old chairs for
the street party. In my father's absence I agreed and helped to carry them
out on to the pavement. Our street looked dead weird without cars and
with flags and bunting flapping about.

50 Mrs O'Leary and Mrs Singh swept the street clean. Then we all helped to put the tables and chairs out into the middle of the road. The women did all the work, the men stood around on the pavement drinking too much and making jokes about Royal Nuptials.

Mr Singh put his stereo speakers out of his lounge windows and we listened to a Des O'Connor LP whilst we set the tables with sandwiches,
55 jam tarts, sausage rolls and sausages on sticks. Then everyone in our street was given a funny hat by Mrs O'Leary and we sat down to eat. At the end of the tea Mr Singh made a speech about how great it was to be British. Everyone cheered and sang 'Land of Hope and Glory'. But only Mr Singh knew all the words. Then my father came back with four party packs of
60 light ale and two dozen paper cups, and soon everyone was acting in an undignified manner.

679 words
The Secret Diary of Adrian Mole aged 13 3/4 by Sue Townsend. This edition Arrow 1982, pages 104-106.

Glossary

pageantry (line 5): impressive ceremonies

cockneys (line 6): working-class Londoners

parasites (line 12): a creature or person who lives on others

dead (line 15): informal adjective meaning very

aisle (line 17): a passage between rows of seats in a church

Kiwi woman (line 29): the famous opera singer from New Zealand, Kiri te Kanawa

sanctuary (line 35): a safe place

cornish pasties (line 39): pastry filled with meat and vegetables

Nuptials (line 52): weddings

Des O'Connor LP (line 54): a long-playing record by a famous British entertainer

light ale (line 60): beer

Reading comprehension

1 Why is Adrian proud to be English?

2 Why did Bert make comments about 'the idle rich'?

3 Why did Adrian miss the actual moment of the marriage?

4 Why did the Singh family come round to Adrian's house?

5 What do we learn about English trains, according to Adrian?

6 How are the local families going to celebrate the wedding, after watching it on TV?

7 What caused everyone to stop behaving in a respectable way?

Vocabulary

Idioms with 'dead'

In line 18, the people at the wedding are described as 'dead famous' and in line 47 the street is described as 'dead weird'. Here, 'dead' is slang and does not have the normal meaning connected with death, but is used to mean 'very'.

The words and phrases on the left below use 'dead' informally in different ways. Complete the sentences using phrases from the right.

i A dead-end job

ii A dead loss

iii A dead cert

iv A deadline

v Dead on time

a is something that will definitely happen.

b is to arrive exactly at a particular time.

c provides no chance of progress and probably pays poorly.

d is something which is completely useless.

e is a date or time by which something must be completed.

Now use four of these words or phrases in the sentences below.

1 As Manchester United are ten points clear at the top of the League, they are a
to be champions.

2 Don't forget to finish your article by the end of the week; the is actually 2pm on Friday.

3 The reason why I want to find a new job is that I'm really stuck in this one – in fact, it's a
.

4 I was worried that the train would be late, but in fact it arrived .

Vocabulary

Idioms with 'hand'

In line 39 Mrs Singh 'handed round' the food, meaning that she passed it to everyone.

Complete the sentences by matching the phrasal verbs and idioms based on 'hand' on the left with the ends of the sentences on the right.

i Students hand in their homework

ii If you hand a book back

iii Teachers hand out exercise books

iv Older brothers and sisters may hand down their clothes

v If you leave something in safe hands

vi If something is off your hands

vii If you keep something to hand

viii If you have a hand in something

a to their students.

b to younger members of the family.

c you return it to the owner.

d to the teacher.

e you are no longer responsible for it.

f it is easy to reach it.

g you are involved in it.

h it is being dealt with by someone you can trust.

Discussion

⊃ Do you keep a diary yourself, or do you know anyone who does? If so, what sorts of thing do you/they like to record in it?

⊃ If you became famous, would you be happy for your diary to be published? Why/why not?

Writing

Imagine you are someone like a famous film star (e.g. Nicole Kidman or Tom Cruise) a pop singer (e.g. Madonna) or a footballer (e.g. David Beckham). Think about what a typical week might be like, and write diary entries for two or three days. Write about 200-250 words.

Unit 9
Legends

The Hound of the Baskervilles
by Sir Arthur Conan Doyle (1902)

The author and the novel

Sir Arthur Conan Doyle was born in
Edinburgh in 1859 and died in 1930. He was a doctor and a sportsman, but he is always
remembered for his famous stories about Sherlock Holmes, the detective, and his friend Dr Watson.
The Hound of the Baskervilles concerns the legend of a huge, ferocious dog which, for centuries,
has endangered the lives of the Baskerville family, who live in a remote part of Devon, in the West
of England. At the start of the story, Sir Charles Baskerville has been killed, apparently by a 'gigantic
hound'.

About the extract

Sherlock Holmes and Dr Watson have travelled to Devon to investigate Sir Charles Baskerville's
death, and to try to protect his nephew, Sir Henry Baskerville. They are walking on the moor – a
wild, open area of high land – when they hear a scream. (The story is narrated by Dr Watson.)

Discussion

⊃ Are there any legends about people or places in your local area, or anywhere in your
country?

⊃ Do you think legends actually have a basis in fact?

⊃ Does the story sometimes get changed over the years?

A terrible scream – a prolonged yell of horror and anguish burst out of
the silence of the moor. That frightful cry turned the blood to ice in my
veins .

'Oh, my God!' I gasped. 'What is it? What does it mean?'

5   Holmes had sprung to his feet and I saw his dark, athletic outline at the
door of the hut, his shoulders stooping, his head thrust forward, his face
peering into the darkness.

'Where is it?' Holmes whispered; and I knew from the thrill of his
voice that he, the man of iron, was shaken to the soul. 'Where is it,

10   Watson?'

'There, I think.' I pointed into the darkness.

'No, there!'

Again the agonized cry swept through the silent night, louder and much nearer than ever. And a new sound mingled with it, a deep, muttered
15 rumble, musical and yet menacing, rising and falling like the low, constant murmur of the sea.

'The hound!' cried Holmes, 'Come, Watson, come! Great Heavens, if we are too late!'

He had started running swiftly over the moor, and I had followed at his
20 heels. But now from somewhere among the broken ground immediately in front of us there came one last despairing yell, and then a dull, heavy thud. We halted and listened. Not another sound broke the heavy silence of the windless night.

I saw Holmes put his hand to his forehead, like a man distracted. He
25 stamped his feet upon the ground.

'He has beaten us, Watson. We are too late.'

'No, no, surely not!'

Blindly we ran through the gloom, panting up hills and rushing down slopes, heading always in the direction whence those dreadful sounds had
30 come. At every rise Holmes looked eagerly round him, but the shadows were thick upon the moor and nothing moved.

'Can you see anything?'

'Nothing.'

'But hark, what is that?'

35 A low moan had fallen upon our ears. There it was again on our left! On that side a ridge of rocks ended in a sheer cliff. On its jagged face, was spreadeagled some dark, irregular object. As we ran towards it the vague outline hardened into a definite shape. It was a man face downwards upon the ground, the head doubled under him at a horrible angle, the shoulders
40 rounded and the body hunched together. Not a whisper, not a rustle, rose now from the dark figure over which we stooped. Holmes laid his hand upon him, and held it up again, with an exclamation of horror. The gleam of the match which he struck shone upon his fingers and upon – the body of Sir Henry Baskerville!

45 There was no chance of either of us forgetting that peculiar suit – the very one which he had worn on the first morning that we had seen him in Baker Street. We caught one clear glimpse of it, and then the match flickered and went out. Holmes groaned, and his face glimmered white through the darkness.

50 'The brute! The brute!' I cried with clenched hands. 'Oh, Holmes, I

shall never forgive myself for having left him to his fate.'

'I am more to blame than you, Watson. In order to have my case well rounded and complete, I have thrown away the life of my client. It is the greatest blow which has befallen me in my career. But how could I know
55 – how *could* I know – that he would risk his life alone upon the moor in the face of all my warnings?'

'That we should have heard his screams – my God, those screams! – and yet have been unable to save him! Where is this brute of a hound which drove him to his death? It may be lurking among these rocks at this
60 instant.'

623 words
The Hound of the Baskervilles by Sir Arthur Conan Doyle. This edition Grafton Books (Collins) 1988, pages 142-144.

Glossary

anguish (line 1): suffering caused by great pain

stooping (line 6): bending forwards

gloom (line 28): darkness

whence (line 29): from where

hark (line 34): an old-fashioned word meaning listen

sheer (line 36): an almost vertical drop

jagged (line 36): sharp and uneven

spreadeagled (line 37): lying with arms and legs spread out

brute (line 50): a cruel animal or person

befallen (line 54): happened to

lurking (line 59): waiting quietly, used here to show that the hound might attack again

Reading comprehension
Multiple choice

In the following four questions, choose the best answer a, b or c.

1 When Sherlock Holmes and Dr Watson heard the noise, they

a hurried to see what was happening.
b ran quickly to escape from the hound.
c fell over as they ran across the moor.

2 When Sherlock Holmes says 'We are too late', he means

a to catch the hound.
b to warn Sir Henry about the hound.
c to prevent the hound from killing Sir Henry.

3 Sherlock Holmes and Dr Watson recognise the dead man because of

a the man's rounded shoulders.
b the way the body is lying.
c the clothes the man is wearing.

4 When they realise that the man is dead,

a Sherlock Holmes blames Dr Watson for his death.
b they both blame themselves.
c Dr Watson blames Sherlock Holmes.

Vocabulary
Ways of looking

In line 7 Sherlock Holmes 'peers into the darkness'. The verb 'peers' tells us that he is finding it difficult to see clearly.

Match the two halves of the sentences below, which use verbs to express different ways of looking.

i The optician examined
ii The tourist gazed
iii The teacher glanced
iv The fans glimpsed
v The little girl peeped
vi The lawyer scrutinized

a the pop star getting into his sports car.
b the document carefully.
c the patient's eyes to see if he needed glasses.
d at her watch quickly before starting the exam.
e at the magnificent view from the mountain top.
f out from her hiding place between the two chairs.

Vocabulary

Idioms with 'spring'

> spring into action   spring to attention
> spring to (his/her) defence
> spring to mind   spring a surprise

In line 5 Sherlock Holmes 'sprang to his feet'. 'Spring' means 'jump'.

Choose the correct idiom based on 'spring' for the sentences below. You may need to change the tense of the verb. There is one you will not need to use.

1 All the soldiers _____ when the officer entered the barracks.

2 No-one's name _____ as an ideal person for the job.

3 As soon as the trouble makers started shouting, the police _____ .

4 He is a very supportive husband; if anyone criticises his wife, he quickly _____ _____ .

Vocabulary

Collocations

i puff and pant

ii take and give

iii go and come

iv moan and groan

v hide and seek

In line 15, the sound of the sea is described as 'rising and falling' not 'falling and rising'.

Two of the following set phrases are the wrong way round. Correct them, and then choose a suitable phrase for the sentences below.

1 'Tell me if you want to be absent from class in future. You can't just _____ as you like!' said the teacher.

2 When the teacher told her students that there would be a lot of homework that night, everyone _____ .

3 After running to catch the bus, the man started to _____ and had to sit down to catch his breath.

4 I used to like the children's game where you had to try to find someone. It was called '_____ '.

Discussion

➲ Have you read any Sherlock Holmes stories, either in English or in your own language? What was the story about? Did it have an exciting ending?

➲ Have you seen any Sherlock Holmes stories on TV or in the cinema? How closely do you think the director should keep to the original story?

Writing

Write a review of a film you have seen. Describe the main characters and say what happens. Say whether you would recommend it and give your reasons. Use 200-250 words.

Unit 10
Difficult decisions

Hotel du Lac
Anita Brookner (1984)

The author and the novel

Anita Brookner is an international authority on eighteenth-century and nineteenth-century paintings, and is also a highly-respected novelist. **Hotel du Lac** won the prestigious Booker Prize for Fiction in 1984. The novel concerns the life of Edith Hope, a romantic novelist, and the decisions she has to make about her personal relationships. An important moment comes when she shocks her friends by changing her mind on the day of her wedding to a friend, Geoffrey Long.

About the extract

Following the cancellation of her wedding, Edith has been persuaded to have a holiday at a lakeside hotel in Switzerland. Having just arrived, she writes a letter to her boyfriend, David, recalling the trip to the airport. (The extract has been divided into six sections.)

Discussion

➲ What is the most important decision you have made in your life so far?

➲ How difficult was it to decide, and did you change your mind in the process?

➲ Have there been any unexpected consequences since making this decision?

---

1 Penelope drove fast and kept her eyes grimly ahead, as if escorting a prisoner from the dock to a maximum security wing. I was disposed to talk – it is not every day that I get on an aeroplane and the pills I had got from the doctor had the effect of making me rather loquacious – but my
5   intervention did not seem to be too welcome. Anyway, she relented once we were at Heathrow and found me a trolley for my bag and told me where I could get a cup of coffee, and suddenly she was gone and I felt

terrible, not sad but light-headed and rather entertaining with no-one to talk to.

10 **2** I drank my coffee and paced around and tried to absorb all the details, as people think writers do (except you, my darling, who never think about it at all) and suddenly I caught sight of myself in the glass in the Ladies and saw my extremely correct appearance and thought, I should not be here! I am out of place! Milling crowds, children crying, everyone intent

15 on being somewhere else, and here was this mild-looking, slightly bony woman in a long cardigan, distant, inoffensive, quite nice eyes, rather large hands and feet, meek neck, not wanting to go anywhere, but having given my word that I would stay away for a month until everyone decides that I am myself again. For a moment I panicked, for I am myself now, and

20 was then, although this fact was not recognised. Not drowning but waving.

3 Anyway, I got over that, though it was not easy, and joined the most reliable set of people I could find, knowing, without bothering to ask, that they were bound to be going to Switzerland, and very soon I was on the

25 plane and a quite charming man sat next to me and told me about this conference he was attending in Geneva. I deduced that he was a doctor; in fact, I had him down as a specialist in tropical diseases, particularly as he told me that he did most of his work in Sierra Leone, but it turned out that he had something to do with tungsten. So much for the novelist's famed

30 powers of imagination.

4 Nevertheless I felt a bit better, and he told me about his wife and daughters and how he was flying back to them in two days' time to have a weekend at home before he goes back to Sierra Leone. And within an extraordinarily short time we were there (I notice that I say 'there' and not

35 'here') and he put me in a taxi, and after about half an hour I ended up here (and it is beginning to be 'here' rather than 'there') and very soon I shall have to unpack and wash and tidy my hair and go downstairs and try to find a cup of tea.

5 The place seems to be deserted. I noticed only one elderly woman as I

40 came in, very small, with a face like a bulldog, and legs so bowed that she seemed to throw herself from side to side in her effort to get ahead, but doing so with such grim conviction that I instinctively got out of the way. She walked with a stick and wore one of those net veils on her head

45 covered with small blue velvet bows. I had her down as a Belgian
confectioner's widow, but the boy carrying my bags nodded vestigially
and murmured 'Madame la Comtesse' as she rocked past. So much for the
novelist's famed powers, etc. In any event I was processed so speedily into
this room (almost induced into it) that I couldn't take in anything else. It
seems quiet, warm, fairly spacious. The weather might, I suppose, be
50 described as calm.

6 I think about you all the time. I try to work out where you are, but this
is rather difficult, surrounded as I am by the time change, minimal though
it is, and the lingering effects of my pills, and all these sad cypresses. In a
manner of speaking. But tomorrow is Friday, and when it begins to get
55 dark I shall be able to imagine you getting in the car and driving to the
cottage.

717 words
Hotel du Lac by Anita Brookner. Triad Grafton Books 1985, pages 10-12.

Glossary

grimly (line 1): seriously

maximum security wing (line 2): part of a prison where dangerous criminals are held

loquacious (line 4): talkative

relented (line 5): changed her attitude and became less severe

Ladies (line 12): the ladies' toilet

milling (line 14): moving around without any particular purpose

meek (line 17): very quiet and gentle

had him down as (line 27): thought he was

tungsten (line 29): a hard metal used in making steel

bowed (line 40): curved outwards at the knees

vestigially (line 45): here it indicates a slight nod

induced (line 48): forced

lingering (line 53): lasting quite a long time

cypresses (line 53): trees with dark green leaves and hard wood, often planted in graveyards

Reading comprehension

Matching headings

a Reaching a false conclusion about a resident

b Making friends during a flight

c Thinking about a boyfriend

d Having dinner with a new friend

e Arriving at the hotel and starting to settle in

f Experiencing an unfriendly atmosphere

g Having quiet reflections at a busy place

> There are six sections to this text. Choose the most suitable heading for each section from this list of headings. There is one you will not need to use.

English in use

Error correction

> Read the passage below, which is based on the text. Some of the lines are correct but some have a word that should not be there.
>
> Put a tick (✓) if the line is correct. If there is an extra word, write this word at the end of the line, and then check your answers with the original text.

0 Penelope drove fast and

1 kept her eyes grimly ahead, as if it escorting a prisoner   _____

2 from the dock to a maximum of security wing. I was   _____

3 disposed to talk – it is not every day that I get on an   _____

4 aeroplane and the pills what I had got from the doctor had   _____

5 the effect of making me rather loquacious quite – but my   _____

6 intervention did not seem to be too welcome. Any-   _____

7 way, she relented once we were at the Heathrow and   _____

8 found me a trolley for my bag and told me where I   _____

9 could get me a cup of coffee, and suddenly she was gone   _____

10 and I felt terrible, not sad so but light-headed and rather   _____

11 entertaining myself with no-one to talk to. I drank my   _____

12 coffee and paced around and tried to absorb all the   _____

13 details, as people think writers do (except you, my   _____

14 darling, who never think something about it at all) and suddenly   _____

15 I caught on sight of myself in the glass in the Ladies and   _____

16 saw my extremely correct appearance and thought, I should not be here!   _____

Literary reference

Not waving but drowning

In lines 19-21 Edith says 'For a moment I panicked, for I am myself now, and was then, although this fact was not recognised. Not drowning but waving.'

'Not drowning but waving' refers to a poem entitled **Not waving but drowning** by Stevie Smith.

Read the poem below. Discuss its possible meaning and then try to decide why Anita Brookner has reversed the words.

Nobody heard him, the dead man,

But still he lay moaning:

I was much further out than you thought

And not waving but drowning.

Poor chap, he always loved larking

And now he's dead

It must have been too cold for him his heart gave way,

They said.

Oh, no no no, it was too cold always

(Still the dead one lay moaning)

I was much too far out all my life

And not waving but drowning.

('larking' in line 5 means 'having fun, often by behaving in a silly way')

Discussion

⟳ Who would you turn to on an occasion when you felt you were 'not waving but drowning'?

⟳ What qualities would you look for in a good friend?

⟳ Can you rely on a friend in the same way as a family member?

Writing

There is a class competition for the best essay entitled 'My best friend'. Write the composition in 200-250 words. You should include a brief physical description as well as details of his/her personality and examples of incidents which demonstrate these points.

Unit 11
A classic heroine

Jane Eyre
by Charlotte Brontë (1847)

The author and the novel

Charlotte Brontë was born in 1816 and lived in Yorkshire, in the north of England. Her two sisters, Emily and Anne, also wrote novels. Charlotte spent some time as a teacher, and eventually married a priest, but she died the following year in 1855. **Jane Eyre** was published in 1847 under the apparently masculine pseudonym of Currer Bell, to prevent prejudice against a female writer. It concerns the story of Jane, an orphan who eventually takes the post of governess to Adele, a young girl under the protection of Mr Rochester. (A governess was a resident teacher with a higher status than the servants in the house.)

About the extract

Jane has recently arrived at Thornfield Hall to look after Adele and has not yet met Mr Rochester. One day, on her way to post a letter, she is passed by a man on horseback who slips on the ice and is hurt. Jane goes up to offer help.

Discussion

➲ **Do you like outdoor activities like walking, jogging, hiking in the mountains or horse-riding?**

➲ **Is horse-riding more popular with boys or girls in your country, or is it about the same?**

➲ **If you have ever had riding lessons, what were the most difficult things to do at first?**

'Are you injured, sir?'

'Can I do anything?' I asked again.

'You must just stand on one side,' he answered as he rose, first to his knees, and then to his feet. I did; but I would not be driven quite away till

5   I saw the event. This was finally fortunate; the horse was re-established, and the dog was silenced with a 'Down Pilot!' The traveller now, stooping, felt his foot and leg, as if trying whether they were sound; apparently something ailed them, for he halted to the stile whence I had just risen, and sat down.

10   'If you are hurt, and want help, sir, I can fetch someone either from Thornfield Hall or from Hay.'

'Thank you; I shall do: I have no broken bones – only a sprain'; and again he stood up and tried his foot, but the result extorted an involuntary 'Ugh!'

Something of daylight still lingered, and the moon was waxing bright;
15 I could see him plainly. He had a dark face, with stern features and a heavy brow; his eyes and eyebrows looked ireful and thwarted just now; he was past youth, but had not reached middle age; perhaps he might be thirty-five. I felt no fear of him, and little shyness. Had he been a handsome, heroic-looking young gentleman, I should not have dared to
20 stand thus questioning him against his will, and offering my services unasked. I had hardly ever seen a handsome youth; never in my life spoken to one. If he had put off my offer of assistance gaily and with thanks, I should have gone on my way, but the roughness of the traveller set me at my ease.

25 'I cannot think of leaving you, sir, at so late an hour, in this solitary lane, till I see you are fit to mount your horse.'

He looked at me when I said this: he had hardly turned his eyes in my direction before.

'I should think you ought to be at home yourself,' said he, 'if you have
30 a home in this neighbourhood. Where do you come from?'

'From just below; and I am not at all afraid of being out late when it is moonlight. I will run over to Hay for you with pleasure, if you wish it; indeed, I am going there to post a letter.'

'You live just below – do you mean at that house with the battlements?'
35 pointing to Thornfield Hall.

'Yes, sir.'

'Whose house is it?'

'Mr Rochester's.'

'Do you know Mr Rochester?'
40 'No, I have never seen him.'

'He is not resident, then?'

'No.'

'Can you tell me where he is?'

'I cannot.'

45 'You are not a servant at the Hall, of course. You are – ' He stopped, ran his eye over my dress, which as usual, was quite simple – a black cloak, a black bonnet; neither of them half fine enough for a lady's maid. He seemed puzzled to decide what I was – I helped him.

'I am the governess.'

50 'Ah, the governess!' he repeated; 'deuce take me if I had not forgotten! The governess!' In two minutes he rose from the stile; his face expressed pain when he tried to move.

'I cannot commission you to fetch help,' he said; 'but you may help me a little yourself, if you will be so kind.'

55 'Yes, sir.'

'You have not an umbrella that I can use as a stick?'

'No.'

'Try to get hold of my horse's bridle and lead him to me. You are not afraid?'

60 I should have been afraid to touch a horse when alone, but when told to do it I was disposed to obey. I went up to the tall steed; I endeavoured to catch the bridle, but it was a spirited thing, and would not let me come near its head; I made effort on effort, though in vain: meanwhile I was mortally afraid of its trampling forefeet. The traveller waited and watched

65 for some time, and at last he laughed.

'I see,' he said; 'I must beg of you to come here.'

He laid a heavy hand on my shoulder, and, leaning on me with some stress, limped to his horse. Having once caught the bridle, he mastered it directly, and sprang to his saddle, grimacing grimly as he made the effort,

70 for it wrenched his sprain.

'Now,' said he, releasing his underlip from a hard bite, 'just hand me my whip; it lies there under the hedge.'

I sought it and found it.

'Thank you; now make haste with the letter to Hay, and return as fast as

75 you can.'

769 words
Jane Eyre by Charlotte Brontë. This edition Penguin Popular Classics 1994, pages 114-116.

Glossary

For words marked * see *Reading comprehension: meaning through context*

stooping (line 6): bending forward
ailed (line 8): *
stile (line 8): steps on both sides of a fence that you can climb over
whence (line 8): from where
sprain (line 12): damage caused by twisting
extorted (line 13): *
waxing (line 14): growing larger
ireful (line 16): *
thwarted (line 16): prevented from doing what he wants

battlements (line 34): *
bonnet (line 47): a woman's hat tied under the chin
deuce take me (line 50): an old-fashioned saying, expressing surprise
commission (line 53): *
bridle (line 58): leather bands used to control a horse
trampling (line 64): stepping on heavily, possibly crushing
grimacing (line 69): *
sought (line 73): *

Reading comprehension
Meaning through context

> Look again at these words or phrases in the text and choose the correct meaning using the context to help you.

1 **ailed** (line 8)
  a something has hurt him
  b something has surprised him

2 **extorted** (line 13)
  a caused him to look around
  b caused him to speak

3 **ireful** (line 16)
  a cheerful
  b angry

4 **battlements** (line 34)
  a the top of a large house, making it look like a castle
  b the gardens in front of a large house

5 **commission** (line 53)
  a ask someone to do something
  b discuss a problem with someone

6 **grimacing** (line 69)
  a a facial expression showing happiness
  b a facial expression showing pain

7 **sought** [past tense of seek] (line 73)
  a looked for something
  b asked for information

Reading comprehension
Comprehension

> Read the extract again and decide if these statements are correct. Put YES, NO or NOT GIVEN (if it is impossible to say).

1 The man's horse is called Pilot.

2 The man is hurt more than he thinks at first.

3 The man is a handsome young gentleman.

4 Jane and the man are in a busy road.

5 Jane likes living at Thornfield Hall.

6 The man knows Jane is not a servant by looking at her clothes.

7 Jane never carries an umbrella when she goes for a walk.

8 Jane finds it easy to take control of the horse.

Vocabulary
Words for 'alone'

alone apart lonely only
solitary single unique

> In line 25 the lane is described as 'solitary' meaning (in this case) that there are no other people walking along.
> **Use one of the following related words in the sentences below. There is one word you will not need to use.**

1 Although Ian spent the evening completely _____ , he didn't feel _____ because he was totally absorbed in reading **Great Expectations.**

2 Since agreeing to separate, Mr and Mrs Finch have lived their lives completely _____ from one another.

3 Cynthia's mother had six brothers and sisters, but her father was an _____ child.

4 This letter is the only one bearing Shakespeare's signature – it's _____ .

5 Alcatraz Prison has special cells where the worst prisoners can be kept in _____ confinement.

English in use/Use of English

Word formation

compel	decide	express	fortunate
pleasure	silence	useful	

Look again at these words which have been taken from the text.

Each word is placed at the end of a new sentence below. Change the form of the word to fit the new sentence. The first one has been done as an example.

1 The teacher told the class that the reading homework was voluntary, but the writing was *compulsory* . (compel)

2 The manager's _____ to pay travelling expenses to the meeting was welcomed by all the staff. (decide)

3 When Margaret was told her exam result, the _____ on her face was one of sheer amazement. (express)

4 The hotel was fully booked up, so _____ we had to sleep in the car. (fortunate)

5 Tim was so _____ that his team had won that he bought everyone a drink. (pleasure)

6 At Christmas we used to sing a special hymn called '_____ Night'. (silence)

7 That old tin-opener is completely _____ ; it won't open anything now – you should throw it away. (useful)

Vocabulary

Phrasal verbs with 'put'

away	off	off
up	up with	

In line 22, the phrasal verb 'put off' is used, meaning (in this case) to decline an offer.

Use the words in the box to complete the phrasal verbs in the sentences below. The meanings of the verb are in brackets at the end of the sentences. There is one word you will not need to use.

1 When I come to visit your country, can you please put me _____ ? (give me accommodation)

2 Because of the snow, the football match was put _____ until the following month. (postponed)

3 I didn't like the film personally, but please don't let me put you _____ going – you might enjoy it. (discourage...from)

4 My teacher is very strict and never puts _____ lateness. (tolerate)

Discussion

⊃ *Jane Eyre* is a classic novel that is often studied at school and university. Tell a partner about a similar book in your country.

⊃ Do you think schoolchildren should be forced to read certain books which are of cultural importance? Why/why not?

Writing

You are entering a short-story competition offering a prize for the best story entitled 'The Meeting'. Write the story in 200-250 words.

Unit 12

A son...

Dombey and Son
by Charles Dickens (1846-8)

The author and the novel

Charles Dickens (1812-70) was the most famous novelist in the Victorian period (1837-1901). Some of his famous novels are **Oliver Twist**, **David Copperfield** and **Great Expectations**. Many of his stories are concerned with social issues, family life and the importance of money. **Dombey and Son** concerns a prosperous family business based in London.

About the extract

The family shipping company of 'Dombey and Son' had been started by Mr Dombey's grandfather and inherited by his father. After his father's death, Mr Dombey eagerly awaited the birth of a son so that the firm could continue to be called 'Dombey and Son' in fact as well as in name. The novel opens just after this event. (In those days, husbands and wives often spoke to one another rather formally, as when Mr Dombey calls his wife 'Mrs Dombey'.)

Discussion

⊃ **Are there any traditions in your family concerning names for boys and girls?**
⊃ **Did your father do the same kind of job as your grandfather?**

Dombey sat in the corner of the darkened room in the great armchair by the bedside, and Son lay tucked up warm in a little basket bedstead, carefully disposed on a low settee immediately in front of the fire and close to it.

5 Dombey was about eight-and-forty years of age. Son about eight-and-forty minutes. Dombey was rather bald, rather red, and though a handsome well-made man, too stern and pompous in appearance to be prepossessing. Son was very bald, and very red, and though (of course) an undeniably fine infant, somewhat crushed and spotty in his general effect as yet. On the brow of Dombey, Time and his brother Care had set some marks, as on a tree that 10 was to come down in good time.

Dombey, exulting in the long-looked-for event, jingled and jingled the heavy gold watch-chain that depended from below his trim blue coat. Son, with his little fists curled up and clenched, seemed, in his feeble way, to be squaring at existence for having come upon him so unexpectedly.

15 'The House will once again, Mrs Dombey,' said Mr Dombey, 'be not only in name but in fact Dombey and Son; Dom-bey and Son!'

The words had such a softening influence, that he appended a term of endearment to Mrs Dombey's name (though not without some hesitation, as being a man but little used to that form of address): and said, 'Mrs Dombey,
20 my – my dear'.

A transient flush of faint surprise overspread the sick lady's face as she raised her eyes towards him.

'He will be christened Paul, my – Mrs Dombey – of course.'

She feebly echoed, 'Of course', or rather expressed it by the motion of her
25 lips, and closed her eyes again.

'His father's name, Mrs Dombey, and his grandfather's! I wish his grandfather were alive this day!' And again he said 'Dom-bey and Son,' in exactly the same tone as before.

Those three words conveyed the one idea of Mr Dombey's life. The earth
30 was made for Dombey and Son to trade in, and the sun and moon were made to give them light. Common abbreviations took new meanings in his eyes, and had sole reference to them: AD had no concern with anno Domini, but stood for anno Dombei – and Son.

He had risen, as his father had before him, in the course of his life and
35 death, from Son to Dombey, and for nearly twenty years had been the sole representative of the firm. Of those years he had been married, ten – and until this present day on which Mr Dombey sat jingling and jingling his heavy gold watch chain in the great armchair by the side of the bed, had had no issue.

40 – To speak of; none worth mentioning. There had been a girl some six years before, and the child, who had stolen into the chamber unobserved, was now crouching timidly in a corner whence she could see her mother's face. But what was a girl to Dombey and Son! In the capital of the House's name and dignity, such a child was merely a piece of base coin that couldn't
45 be invested – a bad boy – nothing more.

530 words
Dombey and Son by Charles Dickens. This edition Wordsworth Classics 1995, pages 5-7.

Glossary

prepossessing (line 6): looking attractive

crushed (line 8): with his head looking a bit strange immediately after his birth

brow (line 8): forehead

exulting (line 11): showing happiness due to success

jingled (line 11): shook so that it made a noise

squaring at (line 14): ready to fight

flush (line 21): a sudden feeling, causing her face to go a little red

feebly (line 24): weakly, without strength

stolen (line 41): moved quietly without being noticed

base coin (line 44): a piece of metal money of little value

Reading comprehension

1 How is the baby being kept warm?

2 How do we know that the baby has just been born?

3 Explain what 'stern and pompous' means in line 6.

4 How do we know that Mr Dombey has had a lot of worries and concerns in his life?

5 What does 'depended' mean in line 12?

6 What is surprising about the fact that Mr Dombey calls his wife 'my dear' after using the formal 'Mrs Dombey' in line 19?

7 Why is it naturally assumed that the baby will be called 'Paul'?

8 Explain what is meant by 'the one idea of Mr Dombey's life' in line 29?

9 What does Dickens imply by the words 'none worth mentioning' in line 40?

10 How does Mr Dombey's daughter feel after entering the room?

Vocabulary

Adjectives to describe people

In line 6 Mr Dombey is described as 'stern and pompous'.
Put these adjectives into the correct sentences. There is one adjective you will not need to use.

> determined   inquisitive   modest   strict   thrifty

1 Mr Thompson is a very _____ teacher; he punishes any pupil who breaks the rules and never gives anyone a second chance.

2 Once Mary has made her mind up, you can't change her opinion, she's _____ to get what she wants.

3 Fortunately, Paul never wastes money; he always re-uses old things and is very _____ .

4 John's baby will get into trouble one day; she's so _____ that she is always trying to see what's round the corner.

> eccentric   extravagant   mean   popular   sympathetic

5 Peter is the most _____ clerk at the bank; all the customers want to deal with him.

6 Tim always understands when I have a problem and need someone to talk to; he's so _____ .

7 Some university professors are so individualistic and do things in rather a strange way; I suppose Professor Jones is like that; rather _____ , isn't he?

8 When Susan married again, she made sure that her new husband didn't spend all their money, as her first husband had been very _____ .

Vocabulary

Verbs for different noises

> chime clatter rattle
> strike whisper

In line 11 Mr Dombey 'jingled' his watch chain. This describes the noise his chain was making.

Put these verbs describing ways of making noise into the correct sentences. You may need to change the tense of the verb to fit the sentence. There is one verb you will not need to use.

1 The soldiers ⬜⬜⬜⬜ down the stone stairs in their heavy army boots.

2 The station clock ⬜⬜⬜⬜ the hour as the train arrived.

3 The church bells ⬜⬜⬜⬜ to celebrate the wedding.

4 'Please mend the window so that it doesn't ⬜⬜⬜⬜ so much in the wind.'

Vocabulary

Abbreviations

In line 32 the abbreviation AD is used for Anno Domini, meaning the years after the birth of Jesus Christ.

Choose the correct meaning for the following abbreviations.

1 P.T.O.
  a please turn over
  b pay tomorrow on-line

2 a.s.a.p.
  a after some action presently
  b as soon as possible

3 N.B.
  a no business
  b nota bene (= note well)

4 e.g.
  a exempli gratia (= for example)
  b easily given

5 P.S.
  a postscript
  b personal supply

6 N/A
  a not allowed
  b not applicable

Think of a situation where each one might be used.

Discussion

↪ In the nineteenth century, sons were often considered much more important than daughters. Has it changed now?

↪ Who do you think contacts their parents more after leaving home – a son or a daughter?

Writing

An international magazine is holding a competition for the best answer to this question:

A woman should choose between family life or a successful career.

Write your entry for the competition in 200-250 words.

Unit 13
...and a daughter

The Millstone
by Margaret Drabble
(1965)

The author and the novel

Margaret Drabble was born in 1939, and studied English at Cambridge University. She has written many highly-acclaimed novels, including **The Garrick Year** and **The Radiant Way**, often portraying contemporary life through the eyes of intelligent, modern women. She has also written several non-fiction works on literary figures such as Thomas Hardy. Written in 1965, **The Millstone** features the life of an unmarried mother and shows her problems and difficulties in an amusing and sensitive way.

About the extract

Having become pregnant, university tutor Rosamund decides to keep the baby and bring her up alone. She has just had her baby and is visited by her friend Lydia, accompanied by Lydia's boyfriend Joe. She then starts getting used to life as a new mother.

Discussion

➲ There are often important moments or 'turning points' in life.

➲ Write down any special moments in your life that have made a great difference to you, and then explain them to a partner.

In the visiting hour that evening, Lydia turned up, with Joe Hurt himself accompanying her. After ten minutes or so, when I had told them as many details about my confinement as they could bear to hear, they began to discuss what name I should give the child. I had spared the subject little

5   thought myself, as I do not like to anticipate, to count or name my chickens before they are hatched, and now I had seen her no name seemed good enough. They suggested names endlessly, ranging from the dull to the fantastic; Joe came down finally in favour of January, while Lydia seemed

to fancy Charlotte, which I thought pretty but corny. After a long debate,
10 they asked me what name I liked, and I said that I rather fancied Sandra
myself. They roared with laughter once more, and all the other quietly
muttering mothers and fathers became silent and stared, glad of a
distraction, finding us as good as the telly.

In the end I said I would call her Octavia.

15 Octavia was an extraordinarily beautiful child. Everyone said so, in
shops and on buses and in the park, wherever we went. I took her to
Regent's Park as often as I could face getting the pram up and down in the
lift. It was a tolerable summer, and we both got quite brown. I was
continually amazed by the way in which I could watch for hours nothing
20 but the small movements of her hands, and the fleeting expressions of her
face. She was a very happy child, and once she learned to smile, she never
stopped; at first she would smile at anything, at parking metres and dogs
and strangers, but as she grew older she began to favour me, and nothing
gave me more delight than her evident preference. I suppose I had not
25 really expected her to dislike and resent me from birth, though I was quite
prepared for resentment to follow later on, but I certainly had not
anticipated such wreathing, dazzling gaiety of affection from her whenever
I happened to catch her eye. Gradually I began to realise that she liked
me, that she had no option to liking me, and that unless I took great pains
30 to alienate her she would go on liking me, for a couple of years at least. It
was very pleasant to receive such uncritical love, because it left me free to
bestow love; my kisses were met by small warm, unrejecting cheeks and
soft mumblings of delight.

Indeed, it must have been in expectation of this love that I had insisted
35 upon having her, or rather refrained from not having her: something in me
had clearly known before I did that there would be compensations. I was
not, of course, treated to that phrase which greets all reluctant married
mothers, 'I bet you wouldn't be without her now,' so often repeated after
the event, in the full confidence of nature, because I suppose people feared
40 I might turn on them and say, 'Yes I certainly would,' which would be
mutually distressing for questioner and me. And in many ways I thought
that I certainly would prefer to be without her, as one might reasonably
prefer to lack beauty or intelligence or riches, or any other such sources of
mixed blessing and pain. Things about life with a baby drove me into
45 frenzies of weeping several times a week, and not only having milk on my
clean jerseys. As so often in life, it was impossible to choose, even
theoretically, between advantage and disadvantage, between profit and
loss: I was up quite unmistakably against No Choice. So the best one

50 could do was to put a good face on it, and to avoid adding to the large and largely discussed number of sad warnings that abounded in the part of the world that I knew. I managed very well, and the general verdict was, 'Extraordinary Rosamund, she seems really happy, she must have really wanted one after all.'

674 words
The Millstone by Margaret Drabble. This edition Penguin Books 1968, pages 104-105, 114-115.

Glossary

confinement (line 3): giving birth

corny (line 9): rather old fashioned

pram (line 17): small vehicle with four wheels used to push a baby in

fleeting (line 20): quick, only lasting a very short time

wreathing (line 27): surrounding

alienate (line 30): cause someone to become unfriendly

refrained (line 35): decided not to

frenzies (line 45): uncontrollable emotions

abounded (line 50): existed in large numbers

Reading comprehension

1 Where is Rosamund in the opening paragraph?

2 Why didn't Rosamund have a name ready for her baby?

3 How do we know that her friends thought that the name 'Sandra' was unsuitable?

4 Why did Rosamund and her baby both get 'quite brown'?

5 What gives Rosamund the greatest pleasure?

6 Explain the meaning of 'she had no option to liking me' (line 29)?

7 Why didn't people say 'I bet you wouldn't be without her now'?

8 How do you know that she finds the baby difficult sometimes?

Vocabulary

Idioms: parts of the body

The idioms below come from the text and relate to parts of the body.
'I certainly had not anticipated such wreathing, dazzling gaiety of affection from her whenever I happened to *catch her eye.*' (made eye contact by chance)
'So the best one could do was to *put a good face on it.*' (accept in a positive way what can't be changed)

Complete the idioms in the sentences below by adding a verb from the box, and then underline the whole phrase. You may need to change the form of the verb to fit the sentence. There is one verb in each box that you will not need to use.

do	give	have
	point	keep

1 All the evidence seems to _____ the finger at John as the thief.

2 Susan seems to _____ a hand in everything that goes on at the club.

3 Andrew was _____ the cold shoulder at the party by his ex-girlfriend.

4 When the boss was looking for someone to blame, Peter told Mike to _____ his head down and try to stay inconspicuous.

put	take	twist	turn	tread

5 James is really insensitive and is always _____ his foot in it by saying the wrong thing.

6 Adrian tried to _____ my arm but I really didn't want to go to the party.

7 _____ heart, Diane – it isn't so bad!

8 Neil, don't do anything without checking with me – you might _____ on the boss's toes.

Vocabulary

Phrasal verbs: intransitive

> come down   come off
> come round   get on
> get up   look up

In line 1 Margaret Drabble uses an intransitive phrasal verb. (i.e. it does not have an object). *'Lydia turned up'*.

Complete the sentences below with a phrasal verb from the box. There is one you will not need to use. The meaning of the missing phrasal verb is given at the end of the sentence.

1 After a long, difficult time things are finally starting to ⬚ for the company. (improve)

2 I try to ⬚ early every morning. (leave my bed)

3 Don't worry about that argument with Susan – she'll ⬚ in the end. (stop being angry and accept the point)

4 My brother and sister just don't ⬚ ; they're always fighting. (have a good relationship)

5 It doesn't look as if that business deal will ⬚ after all. (succeed, happen)

Proverbs

In line 5 Rosamund uses a famous English proverb when she says:
'I had spared the subject little thought myself as I do not like to anticipate, *to count ... my chickens before they are hatched.'*

Match the proverbs below with their meanings, and then check with a partner to see if there are similar proverbs in other languages. There is one proverb you will not need to use. Are some proverbs the opposite of others?

i Many hands make light work. ⬚

ii Absence makes the heart grow fonder. ⬚

iii A stitch in time saves nine. ⬚

iv All work and no play makes Jack a dull boy. ⬚

v Too many cooks spoil the broth. ⬚

a A job is done more easily if other people help.

b You should have leisure interests in order to be an interesting person.

c If there are a lot of people involved in something, it may not be successful.

d If you deal with a small problem immediately, it will not get worse.

Discussion

↪ Do you have any small brothers, sisters or cousins? How easy are they to look after?

↪ What kind of person do you need to be to look after a baby successfully?

Writing

A teenage magazine has invited readers to write an article entitled:

My Mum: The Best In The World.

Write the article about your mother in 200-250 words.

Unit 14
A tricky problem

Captain Corelli's Mandolin
by Louis de Bernières
(1994)

The author and the novel

Louis de Bernières was born in London and educated at Manchester University. He was briefly in the army and then worked in Colombia. His first three novels were a trilogy: **The War of Don Emmanuel's Nether Parts**, **Signor Vivo and the Coca Lord** and **The Troublesome Offspring of Cardinal Guzman**. The story of **Captain Corelli's Mandolin** takes place on a Greek island during a wartime situation in the 1940s, and concerns both personal lives and history. It explores the theme of power and how it is used.

About the extract

This comes from near the opening of the novel, when one of the main characters, Dr Iannis, is dealing with Stamatis, an elderly and partly-deaf islander. Stamatis' wife is also present, and the doctor calls her Kyria. It appears that the deafness was caused when Stamatis pushed a pea into his ear when he was a child. (The doctor sometimes uses over-formal language, medical terminology or French words to impress the couple. These are indicated by an asterisk in the glossary.)

Discussion

When you were a young child, did you (or a brother, sister or friend) ever:

⊃ do anything rather silly?

⊃ have a bad accident?

Explain what happened, and say how the adults reacted. How do you feel about the incident now?

It was undoubtedly a pea; it was light green, its surface was slightly wrinkled, and there could not be any doubt in the matter. 'Have you ever stuck anything down your ear?' he demanded.

'Only my finger', replied Stamatis.

5 'And how long have you been deaf in this ear?'

'Since as long as I can remember.'

Dr Iannis found an absurd picture rising up before his imagination. It was Stamatis as a toddler, with the same gnarled face, the same stoop, the same overmeasure of aural hair, reaching up to the kitchen table and

10 taking a dried pea from a wooden bowl. He stuck it into his mouth, found it too hard to bite, and crammed it into his ear. The doctor chuckled, 'You must have been a very annoying little boy.'

'He was a devil.'

'Be quiet, woman, you didn't even know me in those days.'

15 'I have your mother's word, God rest her soul,' replied the old woman, pursing her lips and folding her arms, 'and I have the word of your sisters.'

Dr Iannis considered the problem. It was undoubtedly an obdurate and recalcitrant pea, and it was too tightly packed to lever it out. 'Do you have

20 a fishhook, about the right size for a mullet, with a long shank? And do you have a light hammer?'

The couple looked at each other with the single thought that their doctor must have lost his mind. 'What does this have to do with my earache?' asked Stamatis suspiciously.

25 'You have an exorbitant auditory impediment,' replied the doctor, ever conscious of the necessity for maintaining a certain iatric mystique, and fully aware that 'a pea in the ear' was unlikely to earn him any kudos. 'I can remove it with a fishhook and a small hammer; it's the ideal way of overcoming un embarras de petit pois.' He spoke the French words in a

30 mincingly Parisian accent, even though his irony was apparent only to himself.

A hook and a hammer were duly fetched, and the doctor carefully straightened the hook on the stone flags of the floor. He then summoned the old man and told him to lay his head on the sill in the light. Stamatis

35 lay there rolling his eyes, and the old lady put her hands over hers, watching through her fingers. 'Hurry up, Doctor,' exclaimed Stamatis, 'this sill is hotter than hell.'

The doctor carefully inserted the straightened hook into the hirsute orifice and raised the hammer, only to be deflected from his course by a

40 hoarse shriek very reminiscent of that of a raven. Perplexed and horrified,

the old wife was wringing her hands and keening, 'O,o,o, you are going to drive a fishhook into his brain. Christ have mercy, all the saints and Mary protect us.'

45 This interjection gave the doctor pause; he reflected that if the pea was very hard, there was a good chance that the barb would not penetrate, but would drive the pea deeper into its recess. The drum might even be broken. He straightened up and twirled his white moustache reflectively with one forefinger. 'Change of plan,' he announced. 'I have decided upon further thought that it would be better to fill his ear up with water and 50 mollify the supererogatory occlusion. Kyria, you must keep this ear filled with warm water until I return this evening. Do not allow the patient to move, keep him lying on his side with his ear full. Is that understood?'

Dr Iannis returned at six o'clock and hooked the softened pea successfully without the aid of a hammer, small or otherwise.

602 words
Captain Corelli's Mandolin by Louis de Bernières. This edition Vintage 1998, pages 2-3.

Glossary

Words marked * are used by the doctor to impress the couple.

toddler (line 8): a young child just starting to walk

gnarled (line 8): rough

stoop (line 8): position bent forwards

aural (line 9): of the ear

obdurate (line 18): stubborn, refusing to change

recalcitrant (line 19): refusing to obey

exorbitant auditory impediment* (line 25): used here to mean something stuck in his ear

iatric mystique (line 26): used here to show that he is trying to impress the couple with medical words

kudos (line 27): respect earned by doing something important

un embarrass de petit pois* (line 29): used here humorously to mean a problem concerning peas

mincingly (line 30): used here to describe the way he imitates the French accent

sill (line 34): a shelf at the bottom of a window frame

hirsute orifice (line 38): the opening of his ear which has a lot of hair

raven (line 40): a large black bird

keening (line 41): making a loud, sad noise

barb (line 45): the sharp curved point of a hook

mollify the supererogatory occlusion* (line 50): used here to mean to soften the object in his ear

Reading comprehension

a Stamatis' wife was frightened about the fishhook. ▢

b Dr Iannis removed the pea successfully. ▢

c Dr Iannis changed his method of dealing with the pea. ▢

d Dr Iannis identified that Stamatis had a pea in his ear. ▢

e Stamatis was told to put his head on the sill. ▢

f Dr Iannis asked for a fishhook. ▢

g Stamatis' wife was told to keep his ear filled with warm water. ▢

> Look at these seven stages of the story and label them from 1-7 according the order in which they took place in the extract.

Vocabulary

Idioms with 'word'

> In line 15 it says 'I have your mother's word', which means that Stamatis' wife was told by his mother.
>
> **Match the two halves of the sentences below, which use expressions containing 'word'.**

i If you are word perfect ▢   **a** you break your promise.

ii If you have a word with someone ▢   **b** you give advice.

iii If you give a word-of-mouth recommendation ▢   **c** you quarrel with them.

     d you talk to them.

iv If you go back on your word ▢   **e** you have learned something correctly.

v If you have words with someone ▢

Vocabulary

Idioms with 'single'

> In line 22 it says 'with the single thought', meaning that they both have the same idea.
>
> **Match the two halves of the sentences below, which use expressions containing 'single'.**

i A single-minded person ▢   **a** are the numbers below ten.

ii If you are singled out ▢   **b** has a clear aim and works hard to achieve it.

iii A single train ticket ▢   **c** you have been chosen, especially for praise or criticism.

iv Single figures ▢

v Walking in single file ▢   **d** means moving in a line with one person behind another.

     e does not include your return journey.

English in use
Register transfer

> Dr Iannis' use of over-formal language might be suitable for a medical conference, but not when talking to ordinary people. The following letter has been written to a friend but the style is more suitable for a business letter. Change the underlined words to a more friendly and informal style.

Dear John

I <u>regret to inform</u> you that I <u>shall be unable to attend</u> the <u>festive occasion</u> at your <u>residence</u> on Saturday. <u>Unfortunately</u>, I <u>am obliged</u> to <u>commence my employment</u> on the <u>identical</u> day. <u>I wish to extend my gratitude</u> for your invitation, and I hope that <u>it will be a joyous occasion.</u>

<u>Yours sincerely</u>

Peter

Discussion
Dr Iannis managed to deal with the tricky problem of the pea in Stamatis' ear without using the rather dangerous fishhook. How would you deal with the following problems.

➲ **You have agreed to help your mother prepare for an evening party, when a friend invites you to go to a disco taking place at the same time.**

➲ **You have arranged to spend a summer day with four friends. Two want to go to the beach, and the other two want to go shopping in the shopping centre. They ask you to choose.**

➲ **Your parents are expecting you to join the family business when you finish your studies, but you would like to be a professional singer.**

Writing
You have seen a magazine competition for the best story beginning with the words:
It seemed to be the most difficult decision I had ever had to make.
Write the story in 200-250 words.